TRAIN YOUR
BRAIN
FOR THE
AI REVOLUTION

**The Proven 4-Step System to
Become Irreplaceable
(No Tech Skills Required)**

DR. JON FINN

TOUGHER MINDS
P U B L I S H I N G

tougherminds.co.uk

Train Your Brain for the AI Revolution
The Proven 4-Step System to Become Irreplaceable (No Tech Skills Required)

ISBN 978-1-0684297-0-5 *Hardcover*
      978-1-0684297-1-2 *Paperback*
      978-1-0684297-2-9 *Ebook*

OUR MISSION

*I created this book because I believe mastering our
Brain States will become humanity's most vital skill for health,
happiness, and success in the AI era.*

*I'll guide you in mastering your own Brain States
and show you how to help others do the same.*

*This book is dedicated to the pioneers who will help
humanity master its Brain States and create an
extraordinary future in the AI era.*

*Thank you for being a pioneer and
joining me on this mission!*

CONTENTS

**SUCCESS CYCLE: STEP 2—PLANNING WITH
THE TASK DIRECTOR**

**SUCCESS CYCLE: STEP 3—OPTIMIZATION WITH
THE DAY DESIGNER**

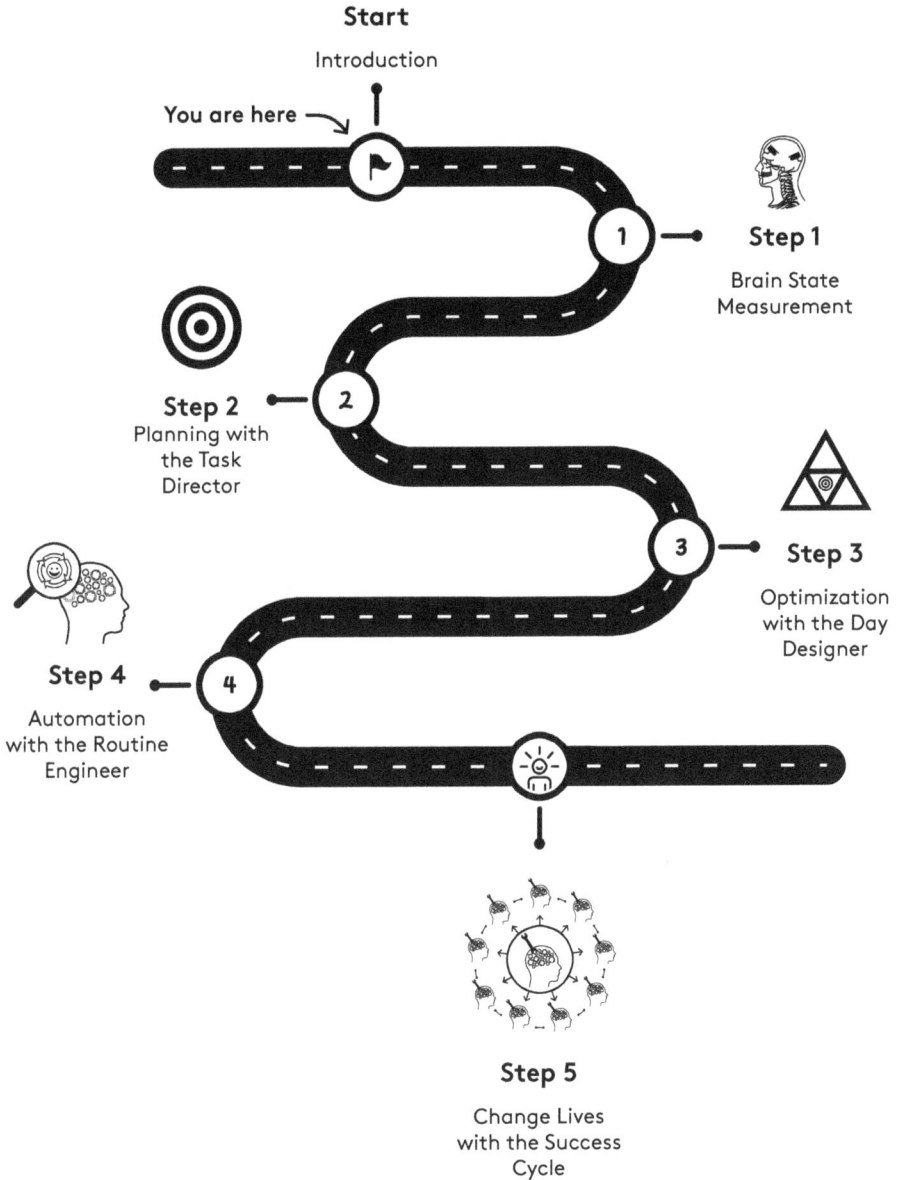

Start

Introduction

You are here →

Step 1

Brain State
Measurement

Step 2
Planning with
the Task
Director

Step 3

Optimization
with the Day
Designer

Step 4

Automation
with the Routine
Engineer

Step 5

Change Lives
with the Success
Cycle

Figure S0.1: An overview of your journey through this book.

INTRODUCTION

HOW TO GET THE MOST OUT OF THIS BOOK

Inside offices worldwide, professionals stare at their screens, surrounded by AI tools that promise to transform their work. Each offers incredible capabilities—analyzing data, managing projects, handling routine tasks. Yet despite all this technological power, many feel more overwhelmed than ever. Something isn't clicking.

To understand what isn't clicking, consider this counterintuitive truth: success in the AI era doesn't require mastering every single artificial intelligence tool. Instead, the foundation lies in mastering something far more sophisticated—your brain, the most complex technology in the known universe. The key is understanding how to optimize your brain's three essential energy modes, what I call your "Brain States."

This book provides a science-based system for optimizing how your brain naturally cycles through different states throughout the day. Learning to match these Brain States to different types of work transforms how you create value in our AI-augmented world. And even if you have not used an AI tool yet, you'll still get a great deal out of this book.

Through our work with over 20,000 professionals—from Fortune 500 executives to world-class athletes—we've proven these brain optimization principles work in real-world settings. Building on the foundation of my best-selling book 'The Habit Mechanic', I've created the 'Habit Mechanic AI-Edge System' to help you thrive in this new technological landscape.

HOW THIS BOOK WORKS

You'll learn the Success Cycle—our proven four-step system for optimizing your Brain States in the AI Era. You can start using these practical tools immediately to enhance your performance and reduce overwhelm. By the midpoint of the book, you'll have everything you need to implement this systematic approach for thriving in our AI-augmented world.

The second half provides deeper insights into the science behind these practices, helping you refine your approach as you gain experience and as AI technology evolves.

Work through the Success Cycle steps in sequence—from understanding your Brain State patterns, to organizing your tasks, to optimizing your daily rhythm, to making improvements automatic. Each step builds on the next.

Keep this book accessible as you integrate new AI tools into your workflow. The opportunities ahead are extraordinary—and they're yours to capture through optimizing how your brain works with these powerful new technologies.

If you have any questions about any area of this book, I am here to help. Just send me an email at:

contact@tougherminds.co.uk

Or contact me via our website:

tougherminds.co.uk

Let's begin with a simple but powerful tool that will immediately make it easier for you to improve your Brain State management.

1

YOUR FIRST 3-MINUTE BRAIN STATE TOOL

Welcome! I'm Dr. Jon Finn. For twenty-five years, I've specialized in the behavioral science and psychology of resilience, performance, and leadership, completing three degrees including a PhD in these fields. My expertise lies in helping individuals, teams, and leaders optimize their cognitive performance during periods of significant change—I've helped over 20,000 people. Now, as we enter the most profound technological transformation in human history—the AI revolution—I'm dedicating myself to helping people succeed in this unprecedented era of change.

Whether you're just beginning to explore AI tools or already using them regularly, the principles in this book will help you integrate these technologies more effectively into your life so you can thrive!

My research has revealed something counterintuitive: professionals excel in the AI era not by mastering every emerging technology, but by understanding and optimizing their brain's fundamental neurobiological energy patterns—which I call your 'Brain States' (more on the science later). Those who grasp these patterns are completing sophisticated projects in a fraction of the time while maintaining energy for what matters most in their lives.

Building on the principles from my best-selling book 'The Habit Mechanic', I've developed a practical four-step system called the Success Cycle to help you master your Brain States and give you the human-AI edge so you can seize the extraordinary opportunities of the AI era.

Whether you're seeking promotion, starting or growing a business, developing your team, or wanting more energy for family life, mastering your Brain States transforms what's possible. As we enter this unprecedented period, technology can either overwhelm us or help us create the lives we truly want—and this system ensures you'll be among those who thrive.

YOUR THREE BRAIN STATES

You have three Brain States. Here's a quick overview:

- **Recharge Brain State:** Your essential recovery mode, when your brain rebuilds its energy reserves

Recharging

Figure 1.1: Recharge your brain daily.

- **Medium Charge Brain State:** Your efficient processing mode, perfect for handling routine tasks

Medium charge

Figure 1.2: Use your Medium Charge brain to complete busy work.

- **High Charge Brain State:** Your peak performance mode, enabling sophisticated thinking and complex problem-solving

High charge

Figure 1.3: Use your precious High Charge Brain State to complete your most high value work.

While you'll learn to master all three Brain States, we begin with your Recharge Brain State—the foundation for everything else. Without proper Recharge, both Medium and High Charge states become impossible to maintain effectively, making it impossible for you to be healthy, happy, and perform to your potential.

Let me share a simple tool that will help you activate your Recharge Brain State more easily.

I will introduce this tool using Sarah's story...

Sarah sat at her desk, her screen filled with three new AI tools her company had recently implemented. Each promised incredible productivity gains, yet she felt more overwhelmed than ever. "I have all these powerful tools," she told me later, "but some days I can barely focus enough to use them effectively. Other days I'm so wired from constant notifications that I can't wind down at night. I can't switch off, can't Recharge. There had to be a better way."

Sarah's transformation began with a simple but powerful tool: the Daily 3:1 Reflection. The purpose is simple yet profound: to help you calm your thinking and achieve what we call the Recharge Brain State—your brain's essential recovery mode. Most importantly, this tool helps you learn to redirect your mental spotlight—to consciously guide your attention away from threats and worries toward more helpful patterns of thinking.

To make the Daily 3:1 Reflection even more powerful, you can activate brain circuits that naturally enhance positive thinking through this pre-reflection routine:

1. First... Choose one (walk or jump):
   - Take a five-minute walk (focus on slow, calm breathing)
   - Jump up and down for 5-10 seconds or more
2. Next... Quickly open and close your right hand several times
3. Then... Force yourself to smile while doing this ☺
4. Finally... Begin your Daily 3:1 Reflection (I'll show you how shortly)

This pre-reflection routine is powerful because it activates your accumbens-striatal-prefrontal cortex network—what Dr. Kelly Lambert calls the "effort-driven-reward" circuit. By using your right hand specifically, you're engaging the left prefrontal cortex, which is associated with positive emotions (your right side activates your left brain). Adding a smile strengthens this positive activation even further! ☺

Ok. Ready to complete your first 3:1 Reflection? Here goes... take a few minutes to complete the following two steps:

STEP ONE—RATE YOURSELF

First, ask yourself this question:

How well did you do your best to be your best and achieve your goals today?

You could say you did great, or you failed. But I'd like you to be a bit more accurate because this will be more helpful for you. So please rate yourself from 1 (you failed) to 10 (you were perfect). You are probably somewhere in between.

Write or type out your score.

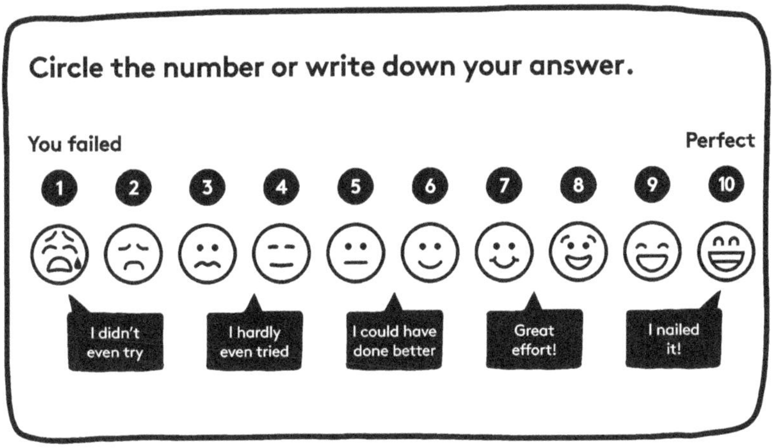

Circle the number or write down your answer.

You failed / Perfect

1 2 3 4 5 6 7 8 9 10

I didn't even try / I hardly even tried / I could have done better / Great effort! / I nailed it!

Figure 1.4: Don't worry if you are not 100% sure about your score; just go with your best guess or gut feeling.

STEP TWO—COMPLETE A FOCUSED REFLECTION

Write down or type out:

- Three (or more) positive or helpful things about your day, and then…
- One area you can improve in the next 24 hours

For example, here's one of Sarah's early reflections. First, here are her three positive or helpful things about her day:

- I am proactively trying to get better at using AI tools
- I had breakfast with my family
- I am doing a 3:1 Reflection

And here is the area she wanted to improve in the next 24 hours:

- Get to bed 10 minutes earlier tonight than last night.

"At first it seemed too basic," Sarah shared. "How could just writing down three positives and one area for improvement help me to be at my best in the AI era? But within days, I noticed something changing. I was calmer. I could see more clearly which tasks needed my best thinking energy. Most importantly, I was starting to understand my own brain's patterns."

Here's the fascinating part of how this works: you're actually using your High Charge Brain State to activate your Recharge Brain State. I'll say that again. By using the pre-reflection routine, you deliberately got yourself into a High Charge Brain State so you can complete the focused reflection and activate a Recharge Brain State. This is what makes the technique so powerful.

I use the 3:1 Reflection every workday evening to process the day, switch off, and prepare for deep sleep. And while it's called a "3:1" Reflection, I actually write down as many positive or helpful thoughts as I can possibly think of. The act of writing or typing is crucial—it forces you to direct your mental spotlight away from threats and worries toward helpful patterns of thinking. This deliberate redirection of attention is the cornerstone of 'training your brain'.

If you want to learn more about the science behind the Daily 3:1 Reflection, I unpack it in Appendix A when I reveal the brain mechanics behind emotional regulation.

But don't worry about that right now. Let's keep going…

Now that you have this tool for activating your Recharge Brain State, you might be wondering about your Medium Charge and High Charge states. How do they work with AI tools? How can you optimize them for peak performance? And how do you maintain the right energy throughout your day?

We'll explore all of this in our next chapter. But first, if it's helpful, make a note to remind yourself to complete a 3:1 Reflection this evening. As Sarah discovered, "At first it seemed too basic. But that simple practice changed everything." Every journey begins with a single step—and this one will create the foundation for everything we'll build together.

2

UNLEASHING YOUR
BRAIN'S FULL POTENTIAL
IN THE AI ERA

Now that you understand how to activate your Recharge Brain State, let's explore how your other Brain States transform your work with AI tools.

Remember Sarah? After mastering the 3:1 Reflection, she discovered something fascinating. "Once I could reliably activate my Recharge state," she explained, "I started noticing clear patterns in my thinking and energy throughout the day. Some hours were perfect for mentally challenging work, while others were better for routine tasks. Understanding these patterns completely changed how I used AI tools."

Sarah had discovered what neuroscience shows: your brain's energy patterns shift between different modes throughout the day. We've developed our '3 Brain States' model (Recharge, Medium Charge and High Charge) to help you work with these patterns, each state being suited for specific types of work.

The science behind Brain States is well-established—as highlighted in the 2023 paper 'Why is everyone talking about brain state?' in Trends in

Neuroscience by Yale University academics. I unpack more of the science and how we developed our proprietary '3 Brain States' model in Appendix B, but right now, let's focus on how you can use these states to transform your performance.

MEDIUM CHARGE BRAIN STATE

Your Medium Charge Brain State is perfect for handling simple, routine, and largely undemanding tasks. For example, sending simple emails, helping a client solve a standard problem, or handling administrative tasks. In recent years, these activities consume more and more of our working hours, leaving little time for premium thinking and doing our most challenging and high-impact work. But here's where AI creates an extraordinary opportunity.

Consider this startling prediction from Winning by Design, a leading sales training company that works with some of the world's largest businesses: Within the next 12 months, AI will enable companies to operate many of their sales and marketing functions at just 2% of current costs while achieving better results. That's a staggering 98% reduction in costs with improved performance! This transformation is possible because AI can now handle most Medium Charge tasks faster and more efficiently than humans, freeing us to focus on higher-value work.

HIGH CHARGE BRAIN STATE

Your High Charge Brain State enables your most sophisticated thinking and high-impact work—from complex problem-solving and creative development to strategic planning. This is your brain's premium operating mode, where your unique human capabilities truly shine.

Our research shows that because of reduced cognitive function (due to the challenges of modern life and what I call 'invisible brain damage') most professionals can only maintain 1-2 hours of High Charge thinking each working day. The rest gets consumed by interruptions, routine tasks, and mental fatigue. In contrast, when people optimize their Brain States, they can maintain 4-5 hours of High Charge thinking each workday.

But here's what makes this moment in history extraordinary: while AI can't replicate premium cognitive work, it can dramatically amplify it—allowing professionals with optimized Brain States to complete 5 to over 6 hours of High Charge thinking each workday. Think of the AI tools you use to augment your high-impact thinking as being like expert consultants who are instantly available on demand, helping you complete your most challenging work in a fraction of the time and at a fraction of the cost. This means professionals can go from an average of 1-2 hours of High Charge thinking each day to 5-6+ hours when they combine both optimized Brain States and effective use of AI tools!

Here's a real-world example. Producing the audiobook version of this book—a High Charge Brain State task—took one person (with optimised Brain States) just 3 days using AI tools. The same task for a previous book of identical length (when AI tools were not available) required two people working for 10 days (20 days in total) and cost nine times as much. That's 17 working days faster and a 90% reduction in costs. We're seeing similar transformations across many professional fields.

A QUICK NOTE ABOUT AI TOOLS

You might be wondering which specific AI tools we used for examples like this audiobook production. However, this book deliberately avoids recommending specific AI tools because they evolve so rapidly—tools available at the time of writing might be renamed, replaced, or obsolete by the time you read this. More importantly, the key to success isn't about using any one specific tool, but rather understanding how to optimize your Brain States to work effectively with whatever AI tools you choose to explore. Ultimately, your journey will involve discovering which tools work best for your unique needs and circumstances.

THE SUCCESS CYCLE:
YOUR FOUR-STEP AI-EDGE SYSTEM

Achieving the type of result I shared isn't about working harder—it's about aligning your brain's natural patterns with AI's capabilities. This is where the Success Cycle transforms everything. Just as elite athletes use sophisticated systems to optimize their physical performance, our four-step system helps you optimize your cognitive performance, and unlock your brain's true power, so you can thrive in the AI era:

1. **Measurement**—Your Brain State Analysis. Map your brain's energy patterns to reveal your biggest opportunities for transformation.

2. **Planning**—Your strategic roadmap. Match each task to the right type of energy and identify where AI tools can enhance your capabilities.

3. **Optimization**—Your daily rhythm design. Structure your day to maintain peak energy for what matters most, professionally and personally.

4. **Automation**—Your excellence engine. Develop triggers and systems that make optimal performance automatic, using AI tools to enhance rather than drain your energy.

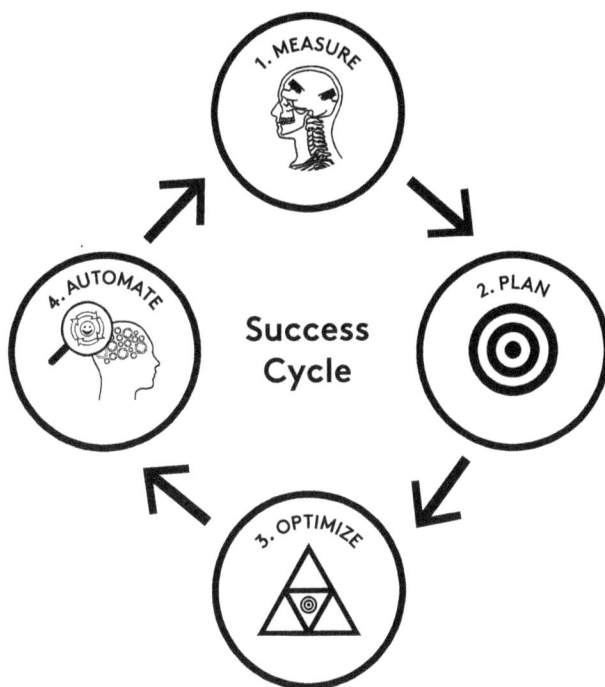

Figure 2.1: The Success Cycle.

The results? More quality Recharge time, less routine and mundane work, and significantly more hours in your peak state—doing the energizing, high-impact thinking that makes you feel at your best.

Sarah's experience shows the power of this system. "Within weeks of starting the Success Cycle," she shared, "I was consistently finishing my most valuable work by early afternoon. AI tools handled routine tasks during my Medium Charge periods, while I saved my high-charge hours for strategic thinking. Best of all, I had real energy left for family time in the evenings."

But creating this transformation starts with understanding something fundamental about how your brain works. In the next chapter, you'll discover a simple story that helps you to begin controlling these complex patterns: the story of your Lighthouse Brain.

3

YOUR LIGHTHOUSE BRAIN

I magine you have a lighthouse in your brain. Two important characters live there. The first is HUE, which stands for Horribly Unhelpful
Emotions. The second is Willomenia Power, or Will Power for short. Most
importantly, Will Power is HUE's guide and mentor.

Figure 3.1: The Lighthouse Brain.

HUE works in the lighthouse's control room. Think of HUE using a beam
of light from the lighthouse to constantly scan your thoughts, your feelings,

and the environment around you. HUE's primary instinct is to spend its time looking for three things: threats from your past (like memories of mistakes or regrets), threats in the present (any immediate problems or challenges), and threats in the future (worst-case scenarios about what might happen).

Figure 3.2: Meet your Horribly Unhelpful Emotions (HUE).

But that's not all. When there are no obvious threats on the horizon, HUE's second instinct is to find easy, new, and exciting things that make it feel good. HUE loves doing things and having experiences that give it short-term gratification.

This isn't a character flaw. HUE's scanning and feel-good seeking behaviors are built-in survival programming that helped humans thrive for hundreds of thousands of years. The problem is that in today's Volatile, Uncertain, Complex, and AI-augmented world, these same instincts often work against us.

HUE naturally gravitates toward Medium Charge Brain State tasks—those routine, familiar activities that provide quick satisfaction. Answering a simple email, checking off an easy to-do item, or scrolling social media all give HUE the immediate reward it craves while using minimal energy.

But High Charge Brain State tasks—those complex, creative tasks that create real value—require sustained mental effort without immediate payoff.

HUE instinctively resists these activities because they demand energy and don't provide instant gratification. When you sit down to write a strategic report or learn a new skill, HUE often tries to redirect your attention to something easier and more immediately rewarding.

This is where Will Power comes in. There's a training room in the lighthouse where Will Power spends time learning how to help you fulfill your potential. When HUE notices a problem or gets tempted by short-term gratification, it can call Will Power for help. Think of it as a mentoring relationship—Will Power doesn't just solve problems for HUE. Over time, it teaches HUE how to automatically respond more helpfully and effectively.

Figure 3.3: Meet Willomenia Power, or Will Power, HUE's guide and mentor.

You've already experienced this mentoring relationship in action through the 3:1 Reflection. This practice is itself a High Charge task that is designed to move you into a Recharge Brain State. It's a High Charge task because it requires focused mental energy. When you first try it, HUE might resist, preferring to check emails or scroll social media instead. But with Will Power's help, you learn to direct your attention deliberately, building something valuable through sustained mental effort.

When you completed that exercise, you were actually using Will Power to guide HUE's spotlight of attention. Instead of letting HUE randomly scan for threats or problems, you deliberately directed that spotlight onto:

- How well you did your best today (rating yourself out of 10)
- Three specific positive or helpful things about your day
- One clear area for improvement

Think about your own reaction when reading earlier about AI's impact on sales and marketing—how 2025 could see costs reduced to just 2% of current levels. Where did HUE direct your spotlight? Did you feel threatened? Skeptical? Now consider your reaction to the audiobook example—seeing how AI tools helped complete in 3 days what previously took two people 10 days. Did your spotlight focus on opportunity or threat?

This awareness of where HUE directs your attention is crucial, but even more important is learning to deliberately redirect that spotlight. That's exactly what the 3:1 Reflection helps you practice. By writing down your thoughts—think of it as going to the gym for your brain—you're strengthening Will Power's ability to guide HUE toward helpful patterns of thinking. Like any High Charge task, this skill becomes easier with practice. What starts as a challenging task gradually becomes more natural as Will Power helps HUE develop new patterns of thinking.

This deliberate redirection of attention creates a powerful transformation. When Will Power can do its job properly, your HUE becomes calmer and more balanced. This makes everything easier—from building good habits around sleep and exercise to staying focused at work and generally being at your best across all areas of your life. As we like to say, "Calmer HUE, better you."

But here's the challenge many of us struggle with in the rapidly changing AI era. Our modern world presents unprecedented challenges that can overwhelm this delicate balance and put HUE on constant alert—draining our mental energy and our Will Power.

For example:

- Constant connectivity (e.g., meetings, emails, phones) makes it hard to switch off.
- Social media triggers endless comparison.
- AI tools promise productivity but create new pressures.
- Constant negative news stories make us feel worried.

But understanding these challenges is just the first step. In the next chapter, you'll discover something remarkable about how these pressures affect your brain's energy system—and more importantly, how to protect and optimize it in our AI-augmented world.

If you're curious about the deeper neuroscience behind how your brain processes these challenges, you'll find detailed explanations in Appendix A. But for now, let's focus on something more urgent—understanding and managing your brain's energy system in ways that transform how you work and live.

4

YOUR BRAIN'S POWER MODES

Your Lighthouse Brain faces modern challenges that go beyond just disrupting HUE (your Horribly Unhelpful Emotions) and Will Power's relationship. In fact, they drain the very energy source that powers your entire system. Let me explain how this works.

To understand how this system works, we need to understand something fascinating—your brain is like a rechargeable battery that has three distinct power modes.

A solar-powered lighthouse (yes, they are a thing!) powered by a rechargeable battery provides a perfect metaphor for understanding how these brain power modes work throughout your 24-hour cycle.

During daylight hours, a solar-powered lighthouse runs on low power—just enough to keep essential systems running while it recharges its batteries through solar panels.

As dusk approaches, it increases to medium power, running low-levels lights that help ships see the lighthouse structure itself.

Then, in darkness when ships need it most, it operates at full power, sending its bright beam far across the waters.

Your brain works in remarkably similar ways. Just as the lighthouse cycles through three different power modes, each perfectly matched to the demands in any given day, your brain also cycles through three distinct power modes to function effectively, and you are already familiar with them. The three power modes are:

- Recharge Brain State: When your brain needs essential recovery and maintenance
- Medium Charge Brain State: When your brain handles routine tasks efficiently
- High Charge Brain State: When your brain performs its most sophisticated thinking and allows you to tackle demanding tasks

Understanding these three modes gives you a unique advantage in today's workplace. While others struggle to adapt to AI tools, you'll know exactly how to match your brain's natural rhythms to different types of work and also reset your brain's rhythms to work better for you. This knowledge is becoming increasingly valuable as organizations seek ways to optimize human-AI collaboration.

YOUR BRAIN'S POWER SOURCES: THE FOUR PILLARS OF COGNITIVE ENERGY

Now that you understand your brain's three power modes, let's look at what affects them. Just as a lighthouse needs proper maintenance of its power system, your brain relies on four key energy sources.

In your day-to-day life, four key sources either charge or drain your brain battery:

First, there is sleep—the equivalent of direct sunlight for your brain's battery. Quality sleep recharges your system, allowing Will Power to guide HUE effectively.

Second is brain friendly nutrition—the special fuel that keeps your brain's battery running throughout the day. When stressed, many people reach for brain unfriendly energy fixes like sugary snacks, excess caffeine and highly processed foods. These give brief energy spikes but lead to deeper crashes, making it even harder for Will Power to mentor HUE.

Third comes movement—particularly walking, which acts like a super-charger for your brain's battery. Being stuck at a desk juggling multiple tasks drains your battery further and also makes it more difficult to get quality sleep each night.

Finally, there are relationships—the social connections that can either energize your battery or deplete it. Constant comparison on social media, lack of time to socialize, and strained relationships turn potential energy sources into energy drains.

When your battery is low:

- HUE's threat-scanning beam becomes erratic, and goes into over-drive seeing dangers everywhere.
- Will Power lacks energy and struggles to maintain its mentoring role.
- Their relationship becomes strained instead of supportive.
- The whole system starts operating in survival mode.

This creates a downward spiral. The lower your battery gets:

- The harder it becomes to make good decisions about sleep.
- The more you crave unhealthy foods.
- The less you feel like moving.
- The less energy you have to build and maintain nurturing relationships.

But here's the good news—you don't need to fix everything at once. You just need to understand how your Lighthouse Brain works and start making small changes to protect and optimize your brain battery.

In the next chapter, you'll discover a remarkable system for getting your Lighthouse Brain working at its best. Let's keep moving on your journey to thriving in the AI era.

5

THE SUCCESS CYCLE

Now that you understand your Lighthouse Brain and how Will Power helps guide HUE (your Horribly Unhelpful Emotions), let's discover the remarkable system you can use to optimize your Brain States and create lasting transformation. This system, called the Success Cycle. It helps Will Power and its three specialist assistants manage your Brain States effectively. I'll use Sarah's story to help you understand how to use it in your own life.

Six months ago, Sarah was struggling to maintain optimal Brain States. Three new AI systems competed for her attention. Notifications constantly interrupted her focus. Despite working longer hours, she felt less productive than ever. Most concerning, she had no energy left for family or personal time by day's end. Her HUE was constantly scanning for threats and seeking quick gratification, draining her battery brain and making it impossible to maintain the High Charge state she needed for important work.

Then she discovered the Success Cycle—a four-step system that helps Will Power optimize your Brain States throughout each day. Will Power uses three specialist assistants to implement this system:

- The **Task Director** helps identify which Brain State each task requires.
- The **Day Designer** creates schedules that recognize and take account of these different states.
- The **Routine Engineer** makes maintaining optimal Brain States automatic.

THE SUCCESS CYCLE WORKS
THROUGH FOUR POWERFUL STEPS:

First comes Measurement. Just as a doctor needs to understand your vital signs before creating a treatment plan, we begin by measuring your brain's current performance patterns. This reveals exactly where you're starting from and what needs to change.

Next is Planning, where the Task Director creates your success blueprint. This step identifies which activities need your premium thinking power and which can be enhanced by AI tools, ensuring every task gets the right type of energy.

Third comes Optimization, where the Day Designer crafts your perfect 24-hour rhythm. This isn't just about work hours—it's about aligning every part of your day to build and protect your brain's energy for peak performance.

Finally, there's Automation, where the Routine Engineer makes excellence an automatic process. Instead of relying on willpower, you develop triggers and systems that naturally guide you toward optimal performance, including strategic use of AI tools.

Then, you repeat the process. The rest of this book will show you how to achieve this, step-by-step. As you master these steps, you'll naturally begin seeing opportunities to help others optimize their own Brain States—just as Sarah discovered when her colleagues noticed her transformation.

Each time you move through these steps, your performance improves. Measurement reveals new opportunities, Planning refines your approach, Optimization enhances your rhythms, and Automation makes improvements permanent. This creates a continuous cycle of transformation that helps you thrive in the AI era.

6

THE SUCCESS CYCLE
IN ACTION

Now that you understand the four steps of the Success Cycle, let's see exactly how Sarah uses this system to optimize her Brain States. Her journey shows how each step builds on the one before to create lasting transformation.

STEP 1: BRAIN STATE MEASUREMENT

"Getting that initial score was eye-opening," Sarah remembered. "It wasn't about judgment—it was about finally understanding what I was dealing with. Once I had that measurement, I could use Will Power and the specialist team to begin optimizing my Brain States."

STEP 2: PLANNING WITH THE TASK DIRECTOR

Sarah knew she needed a new approach to managing her work with AI tools.

By engaging the Task Director's unique perspective, she began creating a complete inventory of everything requiring her energy. This process led to a surprising breakthrough.

"I had this moment that changed my approach to planning." Sarah shared. "I was listing my tasks, expecting to focus on managing AI tools and work projects. But by working with the Task Director, I discovered a deeper truth. Every activity requiring my energy—from strategic planning to quality sleep, from learning new technologies to maintaining relationships—was actually a task needing a specific type of brain power. This wasn't just about time management anymore—I could now see how to optimize my energy for each task."

STEP 3: OPTIMIZATION WITH THE DAY DESIGNER

Armed with this new understanding of her tasks, Sarah turned to the Day Designer to craft schedules that would respect her brain's natural rhythms.

She discovered something profound about energy management that other productivity systems miss: Every hour of her 24-hour cycle either built or depleted her brain energy. What she did at 9 PM directly affected her performance at 9 AM. Her Sunday choices shaped her Monday capacity.

"This changed everything about how I approached my schedule," Sarah explained. "I could see how my evening Netflix binges were disrupting my sleep, leaving my brain foggy for strategic work the next morning. My habit of catching up on emails before bed was activating stress responses that made quality rest impossible. Even my weekend pattern of sleeping late was throwing-off my brain's natural energy cycle."

By treating her entire 24-hour day as an integrated energy system, Sarah completely reshaped her approach.

She designed evening routines to build energy for the next morning. She scheduled AI tools strategically—not just to handle routine tasks, but to reduce cognitive load when her brain needed to Recharge. She even positioned family time to enhance rather than drain her energy, creating natural transitions between work and rest.

STEP 4: AUTOMATION WITH THE ROUTINE ENGINEER

With clear understanding of her tasks and optimal scheduling, Sarah worked with the Routine Engineer to make these improvements automatic. "This step was crucial," she shared. "Understanding task energy and ideal scheduling wasn't enough—I needed to create systems that would make optimal performance automatic. I used the Routine Engineer to develop triggers and routines that protected my brain power throughout the day. My phone automatically goes into focus mode during important work. AI tools activate during specific periods to handle routine tasks. Even my evening routine now naturally guides me toward quality sleep."

THE RESULTS

By actively using the Success Cycle, Sarah transformed every aspect of her life. She now consistently completes her most valuable work by early afternoon. She has energy for evening walks with her husband and helping her kids with homework. She's even started writing the novel she'd been dreaming about for years.

But something unexpected happened as she mastered the system. Sarah discovered she had become her own **human-AI optimization coach**. She wasn't just using AI tools—she was strategically integrating them into her brain's natural rhythms. Her team noticed the difference, and soon she was helping them apply the same principles. Even at home, she found herself coaching her teenage son to use these ideas for his studying.

"What surprised me most," Sarah added, "was discovering how many people needed this kind of guidance. As AI transforms more workplaces, the ability to optimize human performance alongside technology becomes increasingly valuable—both for your own success and as a way to help others thrive."

This isn't just one person's success story. Through our work with thousands of professionals, we've proven these brain optimization principles create remarkable performance improvements. Now, as professionals combine these proven principles with new AI tools, we're seeing even more extraordinary results. It's not about becoming a technology expert. It's about understanding how your brain actually works and aligning that knowledge with AI tools in ways that make unprecedented performance levels possible.

But before we begin measuring your Brain States, let's understand something crucial about why this transformation matters so much. In the next chapter, you'll discover how optimizing your Brain States doesn't just make you more productive—it's actually the key to lasting happiness in the AI era. Then, you'll learn about the same measurement tool that launched Sarah's transformation, helping you begin your own journey to sustained success.

7

THE HAPPINESS EQUATION

Sarah studied her phone, scrolling through another batch of notifications. "I felt busy all the time," she recalled later, "but somehow I never felt like I was actually moving forward. Something was missing."

What Sarah discovered—and what you'll learn in this chapter—is that true happiness comes from a delicate balance.

While part of happiness comes from pleasure and feeling good in the moment, the deeper and more lasting part comes from making meaningful progress in your life—from growing, learning, and developing yourself.

But here's the challenge of our modern world: HUE (your Horribly Unhelpful Emotions), that's the part of your Lighthouse Brain constantly scanning for threats and seeking quick gratification, can become addicted to busyness.

The constant notifications, endless emails, and stream of digital distractions keep HUE occupied but prevent you from entering the High Charge Brain States where real growth happens.

This creates a troubling cycle. Remember how your brain, like a lighthouse, operates in three distinct states: High Charge periods for your most sophisticated thinking work, Medium Charge periods for routine tasks, and essential Recharge periods for recovery. The more time we spend responding to immediate demands and seeking quick pleasures, the less time we spend in those crucial High Charge states where we do the kind of work that creates real progress—the strategic thinking, creative development, and focused learning that make us feel truly satisfied.

Even worse, this constant state of busyness prevents us from getting the deep Recharge our brains desperately need. Poor sleep, rushed breaks, and fragmented downtime mean we're not just missing opportunities for High Charge work—we're actually making it harder to access those states at all. We end up trapped in Medium Charge, handling endless routine tasks without the energy for either proper recovery or meaningful progress.

The promise of the AI era is that we can break this cycle. By using AI tools strategically to handle routine tasks and reduce cognitive load, we can create a better balance across all three Brain States. AI doesn't just help with Medium Charge work—it creates space for both proper Recharge and high-impact thinking.

This three-part balance is actually the key to lasting happiness. First, we need strong foundations: quality sleep, good nutrition, regular exercise, and positive relationships. By helping us complete our work more efficiently and effectively, AI tools protect these foundations in several ways. They reduce the need for late-night work sessions that disrupt sleep, help us finish important tasks during normal working hours, and create clearer boundaries between professional and personal time. This means we can maintain consistent sleep and exercise routines, spend quality time nurturing our relationships, and properly switch off at the end of each day.

Second, we need some Medium Charge activities that satisfy what psychologists call our **'hedonic'** needs—our natural desire for pleasure and immediate gratification. These include both necessary routine tasks and simple enjoyments that help us feel good in the moment. The challenge is that HUE can become addicted to these quick rewards, leading us to spend too much time scrolling social media or handling minor tasks at the expense of both Recharge and High Charge activities.

This is where AI becomes transformative. By efficiently handling routine work like email management and basic research, AI tools free us from HUE's addiction to busyness. We can then consciously choose when to enjoy pleasurable activities rather than being driven by them, creating space for both productive work and genuine relaxation. It's not about eliminating hedonic pleasure—it's about putting it in its proper place.

Finally, we need regular access to High Charge states where we do what psychologists call 'eudemonic' work—the kind of meaningful activity that makes us feel we're growing and moving forward. This includes strategic thinking, creative development, and focused learning. AI not only creates more time for this work but can enhance our capabilities during these premium thinking periods.

"Looking back now," Sarah reflected, "I can see how understanding this balance fundamentally changed my relationship with technology. Instead of letting AI tools add to my stress, I learned to use them intentionally to protect my energy. I had better focus for deep work, real presence with my family, and proper rest. I wasn't just busy anymore—I was growing and actually enjoying my life."

Understanding this balance is crucial because it reveals something profound about happiness in the AI era. It's not just about using technology to get more done—it's about using it strategically to create the right mix of Recharge, routine work, and meaningful progress that leads to lasting satisfaction.

In the next chapter, you'll discover exactly where you are in this balance through the Brain State Assessment. This isn't about judgment—it's about understanding your starting point so you can begin optimizing your own path to sustained happiness and success in the AI era.

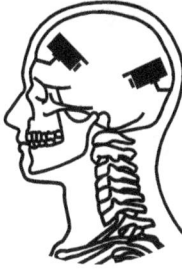

Success Cycle: Step 1

BRAIN STATE
MEASUREMENT

"A journey of a thousand miles begins with a single step."

- Laozi

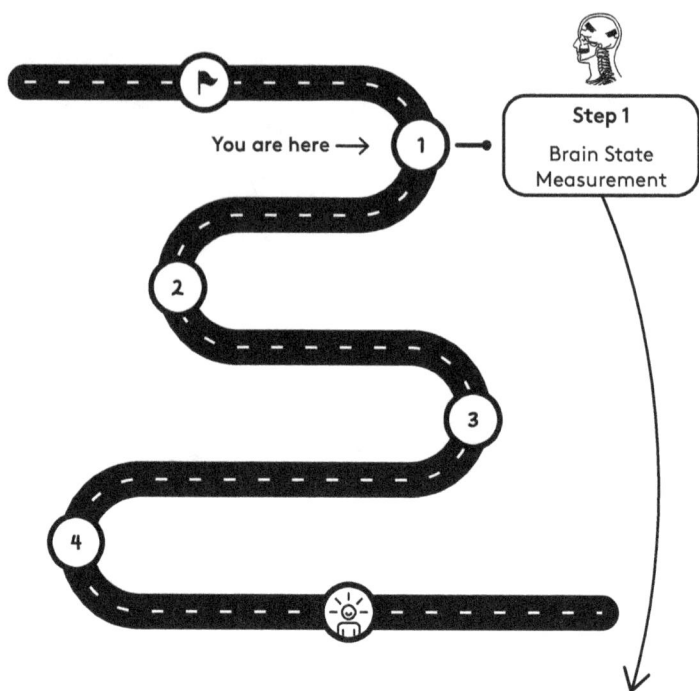

You are here →

Step 1
Brain State
Measurement

Chapter 8: Measuring Your Brain State Starting Point

Chapter 9: Understanding Your Score

Chapter 10: Optimizing Your Brain States for the AI Era

Chapter 11: Why Traditional Solutions Fail In The AI Era

Chapter 12: Like Sport Science For Your Brain

Chapter 13: Your Next Steps in the Success Cycle Habit Mechanics

Figure S1.1: An overview of your journey through Step 1.

8

MEASURING YOUR
STARTING POINT

S arah focused on her phone's battery indicator—15% and dropping fast. "It's amazing," she told me. "When I started working with the Success Cycle, I realized something ironic. As an AI-era professional, I had sophisticated tools monitoring everything from my step count to my sleep quality. I tracked my project deadlines, my team's performance, even my stock portfolio. But I had no way to measure the one thing that mattered most—my brain's capacity to work effectively with all these tools."

Think about your own typical workday. Do you start with good intentions but get derailed by constant interruptions? Find yourself handling endless small tasks instead of doing your most important work? End each day feeling you've been busy but unsure if you've accomplished anything meaningful?

These aren't just productivity challenges—they are signs that your 'Brain States' need attention. Your brain operates in three different states throughout the day. Sometimes it needs to shine at full power for premium thinking work. Other times it needs to operate at medium power for routine tasks. And crucially, it needs proper Recharge states to maintain its capacity.

Without understanding these Brain States, you might be trying to do strategic work when your brain is in a Recharge state, or wasting your peak thinking hours on routine tasks that AI could handle. Even worse, you might be unknowingly doing things that deplete your brain's power just when you need it most.

That's why the first step in the Success Cycle is measuring your Brain States using a proven Habit Mechanic tool called 'The Human-AI Readiness Brain State Assessment'. Through our work with thousands of professionals, we've refined this assessment to reveal exactly how well your brain is operating in our AI-augmented world.

THE HUMAN-AI READINESS BRAIN STATE ASSESSMENT

Take a moment to rate yourself honestly on each statement below, scoring from 1 (never) to 10 (always).

Think of this like checking your lighthouse's various systems—each statement reveals something important about your brain's current functioning:

1. I find myself responding to urgent issues instead of having a plan (or sticking to my plan). *Score:* _____

    Notes: _____

2. I get interrupted (by others, emails/phone, and my own self-doubt/negative self-talk) and it takes me longer to complete my work. *Score:* _____

    Notes: _____

3. I sleep poorly and it takes longer to complete my work to a high standard. *Score:*_____

    Notes: _____

4. I waste time doubting my decisions, second-guessing myself, and beating myself up. *Score:* _____

    Notes: _____

5. My mind feels foggy and it slows down my work. *Score:* _____

    Notes: _____

6. I put off important tasks even though I know they need doing. *Score:* _____

    Notes: _____

7. I feel overwhelmed and I make mistakes that take time to fix. *Score:* _____

    Notes: _____

8. I find myself scrolling social media when I know it is not a good use of my time. *Score:* _____

    Notes: _____

9. I sleep poorly and it makes it harder to spot and prevent mistakes in my work. *Score:* _____

    Notes: _____

10. My mind jumps between tasks instead of focusing on one thing. *Score:* _____

    Notes: _____

11. I get distracted (including by my own self-doubt/negative self-talk). *Score:* _____

    Notes: _____

12. I feel like I could achieve more if I felt more confident and focused. *Score:* _____

    Notes: _____

13. I waste time because I'm not thinking clearly. *Score:* _____

    Notes: _____

14. My diet choices leave me feeling sluggish and it takes me longer to complete my work. *Score:* _____

    Notes: _____

15. Lack of regular exercise (10,000+ steps, elevated heart rate) reduces my mental energy and focus. *Score:* _____

    Notes: _____

Now, write down your total score. *Score:* ____/150

Please note: You can access a digital version of this self-assessment which automatically calculates your score at <u>tougherminds.co.uk/trainyourbrain</u>

This number isn't just another metric—it's the foundation for your entire transformation through the Success Cycle. Think of it like running a diagnostic scan on your most valuable professional asset. Your score reveals exactly what your Task Director, Day Designer, and Routine Engineer need to know to help you optimize your performance.

"Getting that initial score was eye-opening," Sarah remembered. "It wasn't about judgment—it was about finally understanding what I was dealing with. Once I had that measurement, my specialist team could help me create real change. Even better, when colleagues saw my transformation, they asked for help. Walking them through the Brain State Assessment helped me realize how clearly I could now explain these concepts to others."

In the next chapter, you'll discover exactly what your score means and how it maps to specific opportunities for transformation. You'll learn how to create the kind of results you've seen in Sarah's story—consistently finishing important work by early afternoon, having energy for family and personal growth, and thriving in our AI-augmented world.

Your Brain State Score isn't just a number—it reveals specific patterns that will show you exactly where to focus your transformation efforts.

9

UNDERSTANDING
YOUR SCORE

Success Cycle location: Step 1; Progress: 40% complete

Sarah sat in front of her laptop, staring at her score of 95. "I felt two things simultaneously," she told me later. "First, relief—finally understanding why I was struggling wasn't just about willpower or better time management. But then came the crucial question: What could I actually do about it?"

Your Brain State Profile score reveals something fundamental about how your brain is currently performing. Through our work with thousands of professionals, we've discovered that scores typically cluster into three distinct profiles:

IF YOUR SCORE IS BETWEEN 91-150
YOU HAVE A 'CROSS TO BEAR' PROFILE.

Like Sarah, you're probably losing 4-5 hours of premium thinking time each day. This isn't just about feeling tired or unfocused—it's about your brain operating far below its natural capacity for extended periods.

If you have this profile, you're likely experiencing:

- Significant mental fatigue that makes complex thinking difficult
- A constant sense of being overwhelmed, even by routine tasks
- Difficulty prioritizing and making clear decisions
- Poor quality sleep that leaves you starting each day already depleted
- Struggling to create more value in your work than AI could because your brain is operating far below its capacity

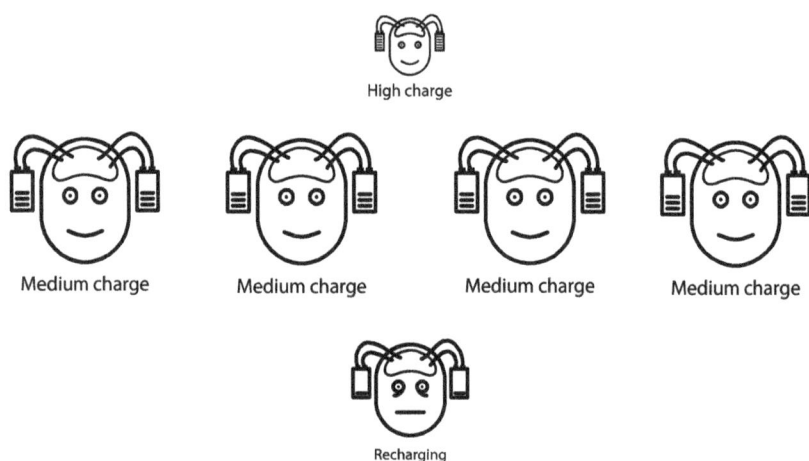

High charge

Medium charge   Medium charge   Medium charge   Medium charge

Recharging

Figure 9.1: A 'Cross to Bear' Brain State Profile.

IF YOUR SCORE IS BETWEEN 61-90
YOU HAVE A 'JAGGED JEWEL' PROFILE.

Think of this as operating at partial capacity. You're likely losing 2-4 hours of premium thinking time each day. Your brain shows moments of brilliance, but maintaining consistent high performance remains challenging.

With this profile, you typically experience:

- Periods of clear thinking mixed with unexpected mental fatigue
- Good performance on some days but difficulty maintaining it consistently
- Sleep patterns that vary in quality, affecting your next-day capacity
- Successfully handling routine work but struggling with more complex challenges
- Creating solid value in your work but not yet reaching your full potential

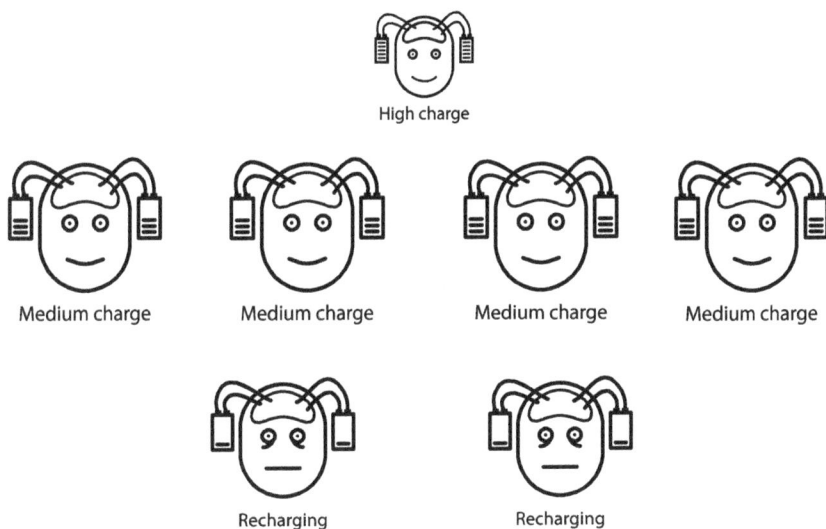

High charge

Medium charge   Medium charge   Medium charge   Medium charge

Recharging   Recharging

Figure 9.2: A 'Jagged Jewel' Brain State Profile.

IF YOUR SCORE IS BETWEEN 15-60 YOU HAVE AN 'ARROWHEAD' PROFILE.

This profile indicates you've established good foundations but still have untapped potential. You're probably losing 1-3 hours of premium thinking time daily. More importantly, you have opportunities to enhance your performance further.

If you have this profile, you're likely experiencing:

- Generally good mental clarity with room for improvement
- Ability to handle complex work but not always at peak efficiency
- Mostly reliable sleep patterns with occasional disruptions
- Creating good value in your work with potential to achieve even more
- Success with some premium thinking tasks but probably not yet maximizing your capabilities

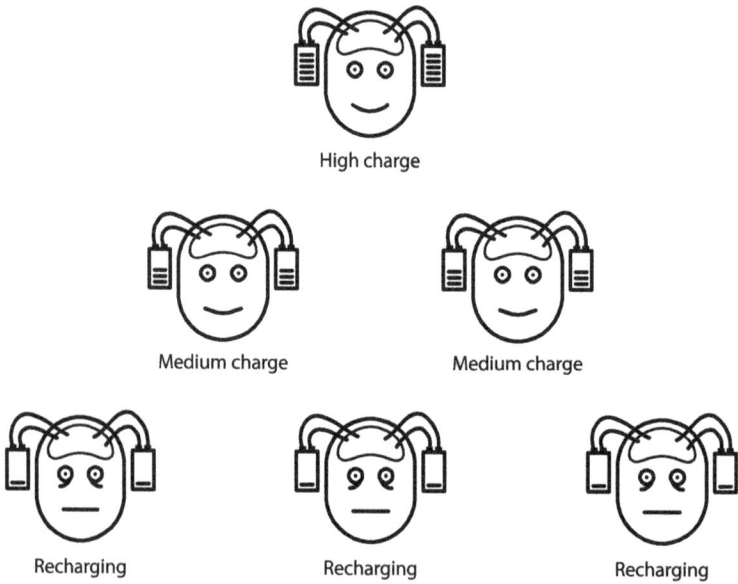

High charge

Medium charge   Medium charge

Recharging   Recharging   Recharging

Figure 9.3: An 'Arrowhead' Brain State Profile.

YOUR BRAIN STATE PROFILE ON A COGNITIVE
PERFORMANCE CONTINUUM

These three Brain State Profiles exist along a cognitive performance continuum. The Cross to Bear Profile sits at one end, representing a brain overloaded, fatigued, struggling, and operating well below its natural capacity. Moving forward, the Jagged Jewel Profile sits in the middle range where optimal cognitive performance remains inconsistent. The Arrowhead Profile sits at the highest performing end of the continuum representing a brain that has established solid foundations for peak performance.

The key isn't where you start, but understanding your current position so you can take precise steps to advance your Brain State optimization and thrive in the AI era. Understanding your profile is crucial because it reveals exactly where to focus your efforts in putting the Success Cycle into practice.

Sarah discovered this firsthand: "Once I understood what my score meant, I could start making specific changes that actually worked. Instead of just trying random productivity tricks, I could focus on a systematic approach to improving my performance."

"But what really fascinated me," Sarah added, "was discovering that these patterns weren't random at all. They were signs of how my brain was actually functioning throughout the day—sometimes operating at full power, sometimes running on reserve energy, and sometimes desperately needing Recharge time. This was the key that unlocked everything else."

Understanding these profiles transforms your own performance—and if you choose, offers a powerful framework for helping others thrive in the AI era. Whether you're interested in formal coaching, already seen as a mentor in your organization, or simply want to help your team adapt to AI, these insights give you the foundations for guiding others toward success.

To help you improve your own score, let's explore brain power modes that underpin it in more detail.

10

OPTIMIZING YOUR BRAIN STATES FOR THE AI ERA

Success Cycle location: Step 1; Progress: 75% complete

Sarah reflected on what she'd learned about her Lighthouse Brain. She understood how HUE and Will Power worked together, and how her brain's battery system needed proper charging. But something still wasn't clicking in her daily performance.

"I understand that my battery needs charging," she told me during one of our sessions. "But how do I know what kind of work to do when? And how do I make the most of my energy once I have it?"

Earlier, we explored how your brain, like a solar-powered lighthouse, operates on three distinct power modes. Now let's dive deeper into how understanding and optimizing these modes transforms your ability to create value in the AI era.

Remember, your brain cycles through:

- Recharge Brain State: When your brain needs essential recovery and maintenance
- Medium Charge Brain State: When your brain handles routine tasks efficiently
- High Charge Brain State: When your brain performs its most sophisticated thinking

Understanding how these states work, and how to optimize them using the Success Cycle, transforms your ability to create value in the AI era. Let's explore each state in detail.

RECHARGE BRAIN STATE: THE RECOVERY MODE

This is your brain's essential maintenance mode—like powering down the lighthouse in the daytime. Just as the lighthouse uses this time to recharge its solar batteries, your brain needs dedicated recovery periods and these work in two distinct ways:

1. Deep Recharge through quality sleep—your brain's fundamental restoration period. Like a lighthouse running on minimal power during daylight hours, your brain needs high-quality sleep to fully restore its systems. When Sarah first started tracking her sleep, she discovered she was only getting six fragmented hours—no wonder her battery kept running low.

2. Light Recharge through strategic recovery periods throughout the day. These moments allow your brain to reset and prepare for peak performance. Sarah learned to take short walks between intensive tasks and practice 'focused reflection' in the evening to process the day's stress before bed.

MEDIUM CHARGE BRAIN STATE: THE ROUTINE TASK MODE

This is your steady-state operating mode, perfect for routine tasks that need consistent but not maximum power. Think regular meetings, basic communications, and standard administrative work. Sarah discovered something crucial about this mode: "The Success Cycle helped me identify exactly which tasks belong here. More importantly, it showed me how to use AI tools strategically during Medium Charge periods, freeing up my limited High Charge time for truly valuable work."

HIGH CHARGE BRAIN STATE: THE PERFORMANCE MODE

This is your brain's premium power setting—and it's what makes humans irreplaceable in the AI era. Like the lighthouse beam at its brightest, this state enables the kind of sophisticated thinking that AI tools struggle to replicate: solving novel problems, making nuanced strategic decisions, and creating innovative solutions that go beyond existing patterns.

But just as a solar-powered lighthouse can't maintain its brightest beam continuously, you can only sustain this state for limited periods—typically 4-5 hours per day when you are optimizing your recharge time.

Here's what makes this capacity even more powerful in the AI era: while AI tools can't replace your premium cognitive abilities, they can significantly enhance them in two ways:

First, AI tools can handle supporting tasks that would normally drain your mental energy, allowing you to focus your High Charge state purely on the kind of thinking that creates unique value. Consider how Sarah used this in her strategic planning work: instead of spending her precious High Charge hours gathering data, formatting reports, and organizing meeting notes, she let AI tools handle these Medium Charge tasks. This meant she could dedicate her full premium thinking capacity to what truly mattered—identifying emerging patterns in customer behavior, developing innovative service approaches, and making nuanced strategic decisions that AI couldn't replicate.

Second, AI tools can help you achieve aspects of premium cognitive work even when you're not quite at peak charge levels. When Sarah needed to develop a complex proposal for a new project but wasn't quite in High Charge mode, she used AI to help structure her thinking—generating initial outlines, finding relevant research, and handling basic writing tasks. This allowed her to focus her remaining mental energy on the sophisticated aspects of the work: developing unique insights, crafting innovative solutions, and making strategic decisions. Through this partnership with AI, she could effectively extend her capacity for sophisticated thinking from 4-5 hours to 5 to over 6 hours per day.

"This insight transformed my entire approach to work," Sarah explained. "Instead of trying to do deep strategic work when my brain was in Medium Charge mode, or wasting High Charge time on routine tasks, I started matching my activities to my energy levels. I began using AI to handle more Medium Charge tasks, which freed up my premium thinking time for truly high-value work."

This awareness becomes crucial because most people make a fundamental mistake: they attempt to perform High Charge work while their brain is in Medium Charge mode, or worse, desperately needing Recharge. It's like trying to run a lighthouse's brightest beam setting when the power supply is low—you'll either fail or damage the system by trying.

The difference between struggling and thriving in the AI era comes down to how well you manage these power modes. Those who ignore their Brain States, force themselves to work against natural energy patterns, and try to do everything at once will eventually burn out. Meanwhile, those who understand and respect their Brain States, match their tasks to appropriate energy levels, and use AI tools strategically will thrive.

But here's what makes this truly exciting: Once you understand these states, you can create extraordinary value while actually working fewer hours. The key is learning three things: First, how to protect and maximize your High Charge hours, which can include using AI to augment your High Charge thinking. Second, use AI efficiently during Medium Charge periods. And third, ensure proper Recharge time.

If you're curious about the deeper science behind these Brain States, you'll find more details in Appendix B where I unpack the central role of 'Activation Levels' and how they underpin your physical and mental energy levels.

SUCCESS CYCLE STEP ONE COMPLETE! ☺

Congratulations! You've now completed Step One of the Success Cycle. Whether you're working to improve a Cross to Bear, refine a Jagged Jewel, or enhance an Arrowhead profile, you now have a clear understanding of your starting point.

But before we move forward, we need to understand something crucial: why traditional approaches to helping people to be their best, or what we call "improving Brain State performance" are failing in the AI era. The traditional methods simply aren't equipped to help people optimize their Brain States, regardless of their current profile. More importantly, you'll discover how the Success Cycle offers a fundamentally different solution.

11

WHY TRADITIONAL SOLUTIONS FAIL IN THE AI ERA

B rain State optimization isn't a new challenge. Even before AI entered our workplaces, professionals struggled to perform at their best. Traditional approaches to improving human performance—from cognitive behavioral therapy to wellness programs—have consistently fallen short of delivering lasting results.

These traditional approaches are even less suitable for our AI-augmented world, where optimizing Brain States becomes more crucial yet more complex. Sarah's experience illustrates this perfectly. Not only was she dealing with the usual challenges of maintaining peak performance, but three new AI systems were placing extra demands on her Lighthouse Brain. Her Brain States were constantly disrupted by switching between tools. Despite working longer hours, she felt less productive. Despite having AI assistance, she felt more overwhelmed.

This reveals an impending crisis that most organizations haven't recognized yet. While billions are now being invested in AI tools and training, three crucial challenges are being overlooked:

- How to optimize our basic Brain States—something we struggled with even before AI
- How to prevent AI tools from making this optimization even more difficult
- How to help people use these tools to make optimization easier

THE TRADITIONAL APPROACH PROBLEM

Those who do recognize this challenge often assume we must have proven solutions. After all, modern medicine can fix most ailments with reliable treatments and predictable outcomes. Break your arm? Medical experts can repair it with proven protocols. But when it comes to getting your Lighthouse Brain operating at full power—improving focus, managing stress, enhancing overall mental performance—the standard approaches are falling significantly short.

Let's examine why by looking at what's considered the 'gold-standard' evidence-based approach: Cognitive Behavioral Therapy (CBT). Most modern coaching, training, and therapy approaches mirror CBT's principles, and CBT has been extensively researched. What these studies reveal is concerning.

The largest and most comprehensive peer-reviewed analysis ever conducted on CBT was published by Professor Pim Cuijpers and colleagues in 2023. It looked at over 50,000 people across 409 studies who were struggling with their mental wellbeing. The results are stark:

- 58% of people who received CBT showed no meaningful improvement
- Of the 42% who did improve, the research revealed that 19% would likely have gotten better without any treatment

In simple terms? Only about 1 in 5 people benefit from CBT specifically. **Remember, this is considered the 'gold-standard' treatment.**

Even more concerning, when researchers followed up a year or two later, they found no real difference between people who had received CBT and those who hadn't.

This reveals something fundamental about how our brains work: Even when people understand exactly what they need to change and are given specific techniques to make those changes, lasting transformation remains elusive.

If traditional approaches struggle to create lasting change in relatively straightforward behaviors, how can they possibly help us master the complex demands of our AI-augmented workplaces? We're not just trying to change a few specific thoughts or behaviors—we're aiming to fundamentally transform how our brain operates throughout the day.

Let's look at four common approaches organizations are currently using to help employees adapt to AI tools. Each of these approaches illustrates why we need something fundamentally different—an approach that aligns with how our brain actually works, not just what we think should work.

1. TECHNICAL TRAINING

Companies invest heavily in teaching employees how to use AI tools. But knowing how to operate a tool doesn't mean your Lighthouse Brain is optimized to work with it. It's like having a sophisticated new lens for your lighthouse but never learning how to keep your beam steady.

2. TRADITIONAL PERFORMANCE COACHING
AND TRAINING PROGRAMS

These programs focus on time management, goal setting, productivity techniques, leadership development, and team performance. They provide valuable knowledge about what to do differently, but here's the crucial gap: knowing what to do isn't the same as doing it consistently. Just like most people know they should plan their day, prioritize important work, delegate effectively, or build trust with their team, they still fall into old patterns. It's like knowing exactly how a lighthouse should work but never mastering the day-to-day practices to maintain peak performance.

3. WELLNESS PROGRAMS

While well-intentioned, these typically focus on stress management, better sleep, or positive thinking. Again, they provide knowledge, but not the system for turning that knowledge into lasting habits. Most people already know they should manage stress better or get more sleep, but they don't consistently do what they know they should. It's like knowing your lighthouse needs a steady power supply but never establishing the routines to keep the batteries charged.

4. FLOW-BASED PERFORMANCE APPROACHES

Again, these are well intentioned, but ultimately flawed in helping us succeed in the AI Era. Flow training focuses on understanding how to achieve those rare moments when we operate on autopilot, executing well-practiced skills effortlessly—for example, hitting the perfect golf shot to win the match, or delivering the perfect presentation to win the business. But in our AI-augmented workday, optimizing for autopilot moments misses the point entirely. Our work now demands continuous adaptation rather than perfection of existing abilities—from engineering AI prompts to collaborating with AI systems. Flow represents just a tiny, elusive slice of our cognitive performance—one that becomes less relevant as these dynamic demands require constant learning and evolution. And even if we understand the theory of achieving flow states, we face the same fundamental problem: knowing how to get into flow doesn't give us the habits required to actually do it.

THE ROOT OF THE PROBLEM

All these approaches share the same fundamental limitation: they focus on providing knowledge rather than building habits. This misses a crucial insight from neuroscience: 98-100% of human behavior (what we think and do) comes from our habits, not from knowing what we should do. Your brain contains over 1 trillion microscopic biological moving parts—including neurons, synapses, and neural pathways—all working together to drive your automatic behaviors. This vast network isn't controlled by conscious knowledge or willpower. Instead, it operates through deeply embedded patterns, which is why simply knowing what you should do differently rarely leads to lasting change. To transform how you work and think, you need an approach that can rewire these neural pathways, not just fill your head with more information.

Think about something simple like maintaining a healthy lifestyle (that is, sleep well, eat well, exercise regularly). Most people know what they should do and have the skills to do it. Yet knowledge alone rarely creates lasting change. We don't do what we know we should do. Instead, we do what we're in the habit of doing.

Current approaches are like trying to learn to drive by reading the driver's manual without ever getting behind the wheel. Sure, you get detailed explanations of proper steering technique, understand which pedal is the brake versus the gas, and know exactly when you should check your mirrors. But without actually developing the muscle memory and creating lasting habits through practice, that knowledge is fairly useless. The same applies to changing how your brain works—understanding what you should do differently isn't enough. You need to rewire your brain's automated patterns.

What we need is an approach that goes beyond just providing information—one that helps us actually build new habits and optimize our Brain States for the AI era. Only then will real breakthroughs happen.

These breakthroughs aren't theoretical—we're already seeing them emerge among professionals who've discovered how to work with their brain's natural patterns rather than against them. But the path to these breakthroughs often begins with struggle. Sarah's experience illustrates this journey perfectly. Despite having access to the latest AI tools, despite understanding good productivity principles, and despite trying various wellness techniques, she kept struggling. But her story doesn't end there. Like many breakthrough moments in human performance, her transformation began with understanding how things actually work, not just what to do.

Think of how sports science changed athletics forever by revealing the science behind peak physical performance. Now we stand at a similar turning point with artificial intelligence—the emergence of AI gives us unprecedented opportunities to enhance our cognitive capabilities. But to seize these opportunities, we need a systematic approach that works with how our brain actually functions—not against it.

This is where the Success Cycle comes in. The habit building principles that underpin it are based on our proprietary 9 Action Factor Habit

Mechanic System, which is (as far as we know) the world's only 'integrated brain-based behavior change' solution, and the world's most advanced 'habit change system.' It stands apart in several key ways.

For example, our TRAIT Habit Loop reveals what truly drives human behavior by recognizing the deep evolutionary patterns that shape our actions. While other habit models stay on the surface, TRAIT helps you work with your brain's natural patterns rather than against them.

Figure 11.1: Other habit loops I have seen did not make perfect sense to me, so I created my own using insights from cutting-edge neuroscience and behavioral science. In case you are wondering, A.P.E. stands for **A**live, **P**erceived, **E**nergy. This is a reference to our proprietary 'A.P.E. Brain' model which I explain in Appendix A.

Then, our 9 Action Factor model provides a complete framework for creating lasting change. Rather than focusing on just a few aspects of habit formation like other approaches, it brings together all 9 of the essential elements that research shows matter most but are actually never considered in one systematic behavior change blueprint.

Figure 11.2: Activating all Nine Action Factors together makes building
and sustaining new habits easier. I will show you how in STEP 4 and
explain each of the Nine Factors in details in CHAPTER 23.

You'll find detailed explanations of these scientific foundations in Appendix C and D.

But right now, let's focus on the positive impact the Success Cycle can have on your life.

12

LIKE SPORT SCIENCE
FOR YOUR BRAIN

To understand what's possible when we learn to optimize our Lighthouse
Brain's performance and get it working with AI, let's recall the dramatic
examples we explored earlier:

First there was the Brain State optimised and AI enhanced audiobook
production that got the work finished 17 working days faster and 90%
cheaper.

Second there was Winning by Design's prediction that AI will enable
companies to operate core sales and marketing functions at just 2% of current costs while achieving better results.

These aren't isolated cases. Among our clients who are learning to combine AI tools with optimized Brain States, we're seeing similarly remarkable
transformations across many fields. This combination mirrors the revolution
that happened in sports performance through sports science.

For example, Sarah, who we met earlier struggling with traditional
approaches, experienced this shift firsthand. Just as athletes moved beyond
simple "try harder" advice when sports science revealed how the body

actually works, Sarah discovered that understanding her Brain States made all the difference.

Before sports science, athletes relied solely on willpower and general training principles to develop their physical performance. They worked harder, trained longer, and pushed through the pain. Similarly, before understanding Brain States, professionals like Sarah relied on working longer hours, forcing focus through willpower, and pushing through mental fatigue.

But once scientists began understanding how the body works and the science behind peak physical performance—measuring oxygen consumption, tracking muscle recovery, monitoring heart rates—the transformation was unprecedented. Athletes could now train smarter, not just harder, achieving levels of performance previously thought impossible.

We're at a similar turning point with cognitive performance. Just as sports scientists transformed physical achievement by understanding the body's inner workings, we can now transform cognitive performance by understanding how our brain works with AI This creates a powerful three-part transformation that can help you achieve your big goals faster than you ever dreamt possible.

First, by optimizing your Brain States, you enhance your Lighthouse Brain's natural capacity. Just as athletes learned to monitor their heart rates and hydration levels, you'll learn to understand and optimize your brain's energy patterns.

Like maintaining a lighthouse's power system, this optimization makes it easier to achieve and sustain periods of premium cognitive performance. Your lighthouse beam becomes naturally stronger and more consistent.

Second, with this foundation in place, AI tools then transform how you handle routine work. Think about all the tasks that typically slow your progress—writing emails, organizing information, handling basic communications.

Modern AI tools can automate many of these tasks, significantly reducing the drain on your system. It's like upgrading your lighthouse's basic operations to run more efficiently, preserving power for when you need that bright beam the most.

Finally, building on optimized Brain States and automated routine work, AI tools accelerate your progress toward big challenging goals. When you're operating in a High Charge state—doing your most valuable thinking work—AI tools can work alongside you, extending what's possible. Just as modern sports equipment enhances an athlete's natural abilities, AI enhances your cognitive capabilities. Your lighthouse beam not only becomes stronger but can now reach further than ever before, illuminating new possibilities while you focus on spotting key insights, developing strategies, and making crucial decisions.

Let me show you what this means in practical terms. Just as athletes using sports science exponentially improved their training, performance and recovery, optimizing your Brain States with AI creates similar breakthroughs in cognitive performance. Most professionals today can only sustain 1-2 hours of High Charge high-impact work daily, with the rest of their time consumed by routine tasks. Through understanding how your Lighthouse Brain works with AI, you can consistently achieve 5 to 6 plus hours of high-impact work while actually working less overall.

Imagine what this could mean for you. Perhaps you're working on a book you've wanted to write for years—you could complete it in six months instead of twelve, while still excelling in your career. Or maybe you're leading important projects at work—you could bring them to completion in half the time while maintaining better work-life balance. The audiobook example shows this isn't just theory—when you combine optimized Brain States with AI tools, you can achieve significantly more while working less.

Picture completing your most valuable work by early afternoon, having real energy left for family and personal goals. Imagine building your business or advancing your career without sacrificing the other parts of your life that matter. These aren't just dreams—they're the kind of transformations we're seeing when people understand how to get their Lighthouse Brain working optimally with AI

Sarah experienced this transformation firsthand. "Before understanding my Brain States," she shared, "I would spend entire days feeling busy but achieving little. Now I complete my most important work by early afternoon, letting AI handle routine tasks during lower energy periods. I have more impact at work and more energy for my family."

This transformation extends beyond individual performance. Just as sports science revolutionized entire teams, understanding how our brains work helps everyone perform better together. Teams solve problems faster because people are at their best during important meetings. Work becomes more enjoyable because people tackle challenging tasks when they have the most energy, while letting AI handle the routine jobs. Most importantly, people feel better at work because they're working with their natural energy patterns instead of fighting against them.

This brings us to a crucial moment. You've seen why traditional approaches fall short in the AI era. You've discovered how optimizing your Brain States can transform your performance. But just as reading about sports science doesn't make you a better athlete, understanding these principles isn't enough—you need a practical system to put them into action.

So that said, let's get back to the Success Cycle. You've already completed Step One. But let's recap the four-step system again so you can consolidate what you have learned and confidently move onto step two and continue your journey to making positive and lasting changes in your own work and life.

13

YOUR NEXT STEPS IN THE
SUCCESS CYCLE

Y ou've seen how combining optimized Brain States with AI can transform your performance—just as sports science revolutionized athletic
achievement. Now it's time to discover exactly how to create this transformation in your own life through the Success Cycle, your step-by-step path
to mastering cognitive performance in the AI era.

Sarah gazed at her Brain State Profile score, feeling a mix of concern
and hope. After struggling with traditional approaches and discovering
the potential of combining Brain States with AI, she was ready for specific
guidance. "Understanding my score was helpful," she said, "but I needed to
know exactly how to use this information to create real change."

This is where your Success Cycle journey becomes truly transformative.
Just as sports scientists use precise measurements to understand an athlete's
current physical performance before designing training programs, your
Brain State Profile provides crucial baseline data about your current cognitive
performance. Like Sarah discovered, your score isn't just a number—it's a
window into your brain's current performance patterns and, more importantly, its potential for optimization.

Remember the four steps of the Success Cycle are designed to create lasting transformation. Unlike traditional approaches that focus only on providing knowledge, each step is designed to help you build the lasting habits that drive real performance improvements—just as sports science helped athletes move beyond "try harder" advice to systematic, scientific training methods.

First comes Measurement through your Brain State Profile. This crucial baseline reveals exactly where you're starting from and what's possible. Just as athletes need accurate data about their current speed, strength, and endurance before creating effective training programs, you need robust insights into your current Brain State patterns. Other performance improvement programs skip this essential step, which is part of the reason why they struggle to deliver consistent results.

Second is Planning with the Task Director—your strategic advisor for matching tasks to Brain States. This specialist helps you develop a success blueprint that goes beyond simple time management to true energy optimization. You'll learn to identify which activities need your premium thinking power, which activities can be enhanced by AI tools, and which can be fully automated. This isn't just about managing time—it's about optimizing your brain's energy for maximum impact.

Third is Optimization with the Day Designer, who helps you craft schedules that respect your brain's natural rhythms and—if helpful—reset these rhythms. Instead of forcing yourself to work against your energy patterns, you'll learn to align your most important work with your peak performance periods. This is similar to how elite athletes structure their training around their body's natural recovery and performance cycles, using science to maximize results while minimizing burnout.

Fourth is Automation with the Routine Engineer, who helps you create systems and triggers that make optimal performance natural rather than forced. This is where real transformation happens—when better Brain State management becomes automatic. Just as athletes develop muscle memory that makes peak performance automatic, you'll develop neural patterns that naturally optimize your brain's performance with AI tools.

"Getting my score was eye-opening," Sarah shared, "but when I started working with the Task Director, I immediately felt like I was gaining more control over my life. Instead of just using random hacks, for the first time ever I felt like I was using a systematic approach to being my best."

Now, let's return to your journey. Having completed Step 1, you're ready to begin Step 2 with the Task Director. In the next chapter, you'll discover one of their most powerful tools—your Future Ambitious Meaningful Story. This process will help you connect your current reality with your greatest potential, creating a clear path forward just as it did for Sarah. But first, take a moment to appreciate how far you've come. By measuring your Brain States, you've taken the essential first step toward mastering your performance in the AI era. More importantly, you've begun a journey that can transform not only your work but your entire life.

Success Cycle: Step 2
PLANNING WITH THE TASK DIRECTOR

"The foundation determines the height."

- Task Director

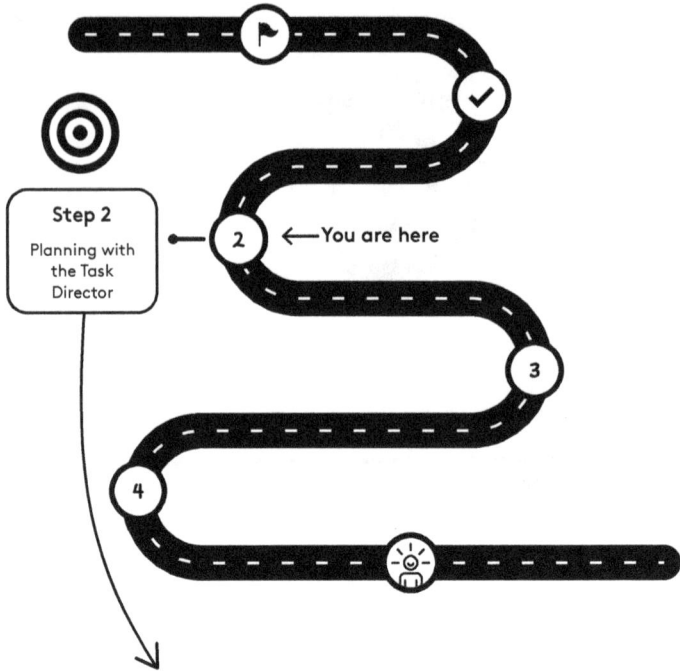

Step 2

Planning with the Task Director

←You are here

Chapter 14: Creating Your Future Vision

Chapter 15: Creating Your FAM Story with the Task Director

Chapter 16: Breaking Down Your FAM Journey: The Step-by-Step Action Plan

Chapter 17: Building Your Foundation for Success

Chapter 18: Measuring and Strengthening Your Foundation

Chapter 19: Organizing Your Priority Tasks for the Next 30 days

Figure S2.1: An overview of your journey through Step 2.

14

CREATING YOUR FUTURE VISION

S arah sat in her favorite coffee shop, a notebook open before her. "I had my Brain State Profile score," she explained, "but I kept asking myself—what am I really trying to optimize my Brain States for? What future am I trying to create?"

This is where you'll use one of the Task Director's most powerful tools: the Future Ambitious Meaningful (FAM) Story. Just as a lighthouse's beam guides ships through darkness, your FAM Story helps direct your brain's energy toward meaningful long-term goals while managing your states day by day.

"Working with the Task Director helped me discover something crucial," Sarah shared. "My Brain State Profile wasn't just showing me my current performance—it was revealing the gap between my present Brain States and the ones I needed to achieve my biggest goals. Creating my FAM Story helped me see exactly how to use the Success Cycle to close that gap."

Think of your FAM Story like an iceberg. The visible tip represents your long-term vision—where you want to be in ten years or so. Just above the surface are your medium-term goals for the next one to four years. Underwater are your twelve-month objectives. Then deeper underwater are your monthly targets, weekly priorities, and daily actions. Each layer connects your present Brain States to your future ambitions.

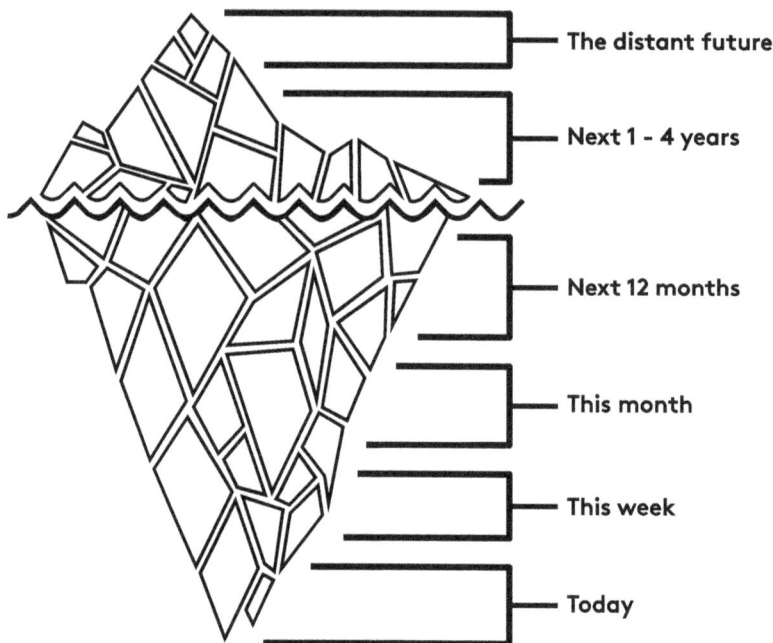

Figure 14.1: The FAM Story Iceberg helps you understand and better control the impact your daily habits have on your health, happiness, and performance in the future.

The power of your FAM Story comes from how it creates what we call a "wave of motivation." This helps direct your brain's energy and Will Power's efforts in three powerful ways:

First, it helps you track progress. Research shows the single biggest cause of burnout isn't overload—it's working too long without experiencing personal progress. Your FAM Story lets you see the weekly, monthly and yearly progress you are making in your life, all driven by Brain State optimization.

Second, it helps manage stress. Setting and monitoring goals makes it easier to reset and recalibrate when we falter. When set correctly, goals become powerful stress management tools. They're meant to be adjusted and refined as you progress or fail to progress—serving as adaptable signposts that help Will Power and its specialists optimize your journey.

Third, your FAM Story creates self-fulfilling prophecies. Walt Disney famously said: "If you can dream it, you can do it." Columbia University Professor Robert Merton's research showed that believing you can achieve something, significantly increases your chances of success. Your FAM Story helps Will Power guide HUE (your Horribly Unhelpful Emotions) toward positive behavioral patterns aligned with your ambitions—making it easier to optimize your Brain States today because you can clearly see how it will help you create a better tomorrow.

"The Task Director helped me understand something powerful," Sarah explained. "Every time I updated my FAM Story—usually every 4-8 weeks—I could see more clearly how managing my Brain States connected to my bigger goals. Better sleep wasn't just about feeling less tired—it was about having the High Charge brain power to write my novel. Using AI tools effectively wasn't just about productivity—it was about creating space and energy for what mattered most."

Sarah discovered something else too: "As I mastered this process, I found myself naturally helping colleagues create their own FAM Stories. There's something powerful about helping others connect their daily Brain States to their biggest dreams."

In the next chapter, you'll learn exactly how to create your own FAM Story with the Task Director. You'll discover how to connect your Brain State Profile to your future vision through specific questions and exercises. Just as Sarah used this tool to transform her performance, you'll see how optimizing your Brain States today shapes the future you want to create.

15

CREATING YOUR FAM STORY WITH THE TASK DIRECTOR

Success Cycle location: Step 2; Progress: 20% complete

L et's discover how to use the Task Director to create your FAM Story—the tool that will connect your Brain State Profile to your future vision. Just as Sarah used this process to transform her wellbeing and performance, you'll learn how to map out your journey from current Brain States to you consistently being at your very best.

To make it easier to create your FAM Story, I have created a PDF template to guide you through the exercises in this chapter and the next chapter. Go to tougherminds.co.uk/trainyourbrain to download your copy.

First, the Task Director will help you think about who inspires you. "This was eye-opening," Sarah shared. "I started listing people I admired—from famous leaders to authors who have walked the path I want to follow. Looking at their patterns helped me see what Brain States I needed to cultivate."

Write down your answers to the following questions:

1. THINK ABOUT WHO INSPIRES YOU? BE SPECIFIC AND NAME NAMES.

Some ideas (in no particular order) to spark your thoughts:

- Parents
- Siblings
- Grandparents
- Family
- Colleagues
- People who have changed society
- Scientists
- Nobel Prize winners
- Entrepreneurs
- Mentors
- Writers
- Sporting champions
- Political leaders
- High achievers
- Musicians, artists and other creative people

If you're not sure, start by thinking about the kind of people who don't inspire you.

2. THINK ABOUT WHY THE PEOPLE WHO INSPIRE YOU ACTUALLY INSPIRE YOU? (BE SPECIFIC. IDENTIFY THEIR SHARED AND INDIVIDUAL QUALITIES.)

Some ideas (in no particular order) to spark your thoughts:

- Dedication
- Persistence
- Self-sacrifice
- Determination
- Desire
- Work ethic
- Success
- Tolerance
- Progress
- Excellence
- Innovation
- Humility
- Dependability
- Resilience
- Attitude
- Guts

3. THINK ABOUT WHAT YOU DO TO FEEL AT YOUR BEST—HERE ARE SOME EXAMPLES:

- Have fun
- Help others
- Develop myself
- Relax
- Do meaningful work
- Show humility
- Give my best
- Have a good work-life balance

- Achieve results
- Be dedicated
- Be determined
- Persist with difficult challenges
- Be resilient
- Show the right attitude
- Make personal progress
- Be diligent
- Be dependable
- Be tolerant
- Eat well
- Sleep well
- Show self-control

4. THINK ABOUT WHY IS IT IMPORTANT FOR YOU TO DO THESE THINGS, AND WHAT OUTCOMES DO THEY HELP YOU ACHIEVE?

5. THINK ABOUT YOUR TOP STRENGTHS.

Here are some ideas (in no particular order) to spark your thoughts:

- Dedication
- Desire
- Persistence
- Self-sacrifice
- Positive attitude

- Calm
- Work ethic
- Reflective
- Success
- Humility
- Tolerance
- Diligence
- Dependability
- Excellence
- Attitude
- Innovative

6. THINK ABOUT THE MOST IMPORTANT AND DIFFICULT THINGS YOU HAVE ACHIEVED IN YOUR LIFE SO FAR, OR IN THE PAST 12 MONTHS.

7. THINK ABOUT HOW YOU MANAGED TO BE PERSISTENT TO SECURE THIS ACHIEVEMENT.

"Although I knew I didn't have perfect answers for all of these areas, just thinking about these things was crucial," Sarah explained. "I started seeing the connection between my role models, strengths, best moments and the type of person I wanted to be in the future."

Congratulations! With these insights, you're ready to build your FAM Story Iceberg.

16

BREAKING DOWN YOUR FAM JOURNEY: THE STEP-BY-STEP ACTION PLAN

◎ Success Cycle location: Step 2; Progress: 40% complete

Now that you've explored your inspirations and reflected on your strengths, it's time to transform these insights into a practical plan. The Task Director will guide you through creating a detailed roadmap that connects your Brain States to your biggest goals.

The FAM Form provides a systematic approach to this planning process. You'll learn how to break down your long-term vision into specific actions that optimize your Brain States day-by-day. This creates a clear line of sight from your future ambitions to your daily choices.

As Sarah discovered, this planning process brings clarity to every level of your journey: "Once I had my complete FAM Story, I could see exactly how managing my Brain States today would help me achieve my ten-year vision. Each daily action became a meaningful step toward my bigger goals."

Broadly, the FAM Form makes you think about the future and present in the following terms:

- What do I want to achieve in the distant future?
- What do I need to do in the next **one** to **four years** to achieve my distant future goals?
- To achieve the above, what do I need to achieve in the next **12 months**?
- To achieve the above, what do I need to achieve in the next **6 months**?
- To achieve the above, what do I need to achieve in the next **3 months**?
- To achieve the above, what do I need to achieve in the next **30 days**?
- To achieve the above, what do I need to achieve **this week**?
- To achieve the above, what do I need to prioritize **today**?

Sometimes we might feel reluctant to commit to achieving a major, long-term objective. But the beauty of the FAM Form is that it allows us to be flexible. We can decide to pivot and change our goals. They are not set in stone.

I encourage everyone who wants to be their best to periodically think about their own long-term goals. I step back to reflect and use the FAM Form to update my FAM Story every four to eight weeks. My FAM Story goals change because my life circumstances change.

Sometimes the changes to my goals are tiny, and sometimes they are big. But what is most important is that I am engaging in a purposeful reflection and planning process. This helps me learn about myself and how to be at my best.

"The FAM Form helped me see how it all connected," Sarah shared. "My 10-year vision included writing a novel while maintaining a thriving career and family life. That meant optimizing my High Charge states for creative work, using AI tools effectively in Medium Charge periods, and mastering my Recharge patterns. Each layer of the iceberg showed me exactly what to work on next."

Here are the FAM Form Questions to Help You Create Your Own FAM Story. Remember, the answers you give and the goals you set are not set in stone. They are flexible and can be changed at any time to make them more helpful for you.

1. THINK ABOUT WHAT YOU'D LIKE TO BE DOING AND WHAT YOU'D LIKE TO HAVE IN THE MEDIUM TO DISTANT FUTURE (E.G., 10 YEARS OR MORE)?

Some words to get you thinking about your future goals:

- Location
- Family
- Possessions
- Friends and relationships
- Health
- Home
- Money
- Roles and responsibilities
- Job

Tip: If you are not sure, start by thinking about what you DO NOT want your future to look like.

Developing your long-term goals will take time. The aim of this exercise is not to create perfect goals but to get you thinking and started on your journey to having a clearer understanding about what you want your future self and life to look like. Remember, whatever you write down can be changed.

Should you set goals that might feel unrealistic?

I do because I have found that even if I do not achieve these goals, having a high level of expectation is helpful. It means I achieve a higher level of happiness and performance than I would have if I'd set myself less ambitious goals. This is something I have learned through practice.

Should you make an exact copy of my approach?

No! You need to develop an approach that works best for you. You will only work out the best way to set the type of goals that work best for you by trying things out. Goals are powerful tools, but it can take a lot of trial and error to learn how to use them effectively.

Why × 5?

To make your long-term goals more meaningful and powerful, try to understand "Why?" you want to achieve them. An effective way to do this is to ask yourself "Why?" five times.

For example, if you want to get a promotion at work, you might ask yourself "Why?" The answer might be, "Because you want to earn more money."

So you would then ask yourself, why do you want to earn more money? That answer might be, "Because you want to move to a bigger house."

Then, you would ask yourself, why do you want to live in a bigger house? This answer could be, "So my young children have a garden to play in."

The next question you might ask yourself is why is it important for you to have a garden your children can play in? The answer could be, "I understand the importance of outdoor play for healthy development and I want to provide a space at home where they can do this."

By the time you have asked yourself "Why?" at least five times, you will develop a clear understanding of the deeper reasons for your goals and ambitions. The more meaningful your reasons for wanting to achieve a goal, the more powerful they will be in helping you persist and succeed.

Now, let's get back to our FAM Form questions.

2. THINK ABOUT WHAT YOU NEED TO ACHIEVE IN THE NEXT **ONE** TO **FOUR YEARS** TO MAKE YOUR DISTANT/ MEDIUM FUTURE GOALS ATTAINABLE?

3. THINK ABOUT WHAT YOU NEED TO ACHIEVE IN THE NEXT **12 MONTHS** TO MAKE YOUR ONE-TO-FOUR-YEAR GOALS ATTAINABLE?

4. THINK ABOUT WHAT YOU NEED TO ACHIEVE IN THE NEXT 6 MONTHS TO MAKE YOUR 12 MONTH GOALS ATTAINABLE?

_____

_____

_____

5. THINK ABOUT WHAT YOU NEED TO ACHIEVE IN THE NEXT 3 MONTHS TO MAKE YOUR 6 MONTH GOALS ATTAINABLE?

_____

_____

_____

With your long-term FAM Story taking shape, you're ready to discover how these aspirations translate into daily actions. In the next chapter, we'll explore the foundational habits that will turn your vision into reality—the daily practices that optimize your Brain States and steadily move you toward your goals.

17

BUILDING YOUR FOUNDATION FOR SUCCESS

Success Cycle location: Step 2; Progress: 60% complete

Now that you've created your long-term vision with the Task Director through your FAM Story, it's time to focus on something crucial—the daily habits that will build your path to that future. As Sarah discovered, transforming your Brain States isn't just about big goals—it's also about the small, consistent actions that create lasting change.

"Creating my FAM Story was exciting," Sarah shared, "but the Task Director helped me see something important. I needed to strengthen my foundation before I could reach those bigger goals. That meant focusing on basic habits that would optimize my Brain States day by day."

Think of these foundational habits like the base of your lighthouse. Just as a lighthouse needs a solid foundation to maintain its structure during rough seas and storms, your brain needs core habits that maintain optimal states through daily challenges. Here are six key areas that need your attention:

1. **Sleep**—Your brain's primary Recharge mechanism. Quality sleep isn't just about feeling better - it's essential for maintaining the High Charge states you need for premium thinking work.

2. **Diet**—The fuel for your brain's energy system. What and when you eat directly affects your ability to maintain optimal Brain States throughout the day.

3. **Exercise**—Your brain's natural energy optimizer. Regular movement, especially walking, helps regulate your Brain States and enhance your capacity for both High Charge thinking and proper Recharge.

4. **Stress Management**—Your brain's balance system. Managing stress effectively helps prevent HUE from becoming overactive and draining your energy unnecessarily.

5. **Confidence**—Your performance foundation. Building and maintaining confidence helps you tackle challenges while maintaining optimal Brain States.

6. **Focus, impact and productivity**—Your daily effectiveness system. Having clear routines and systems helps you match tasks to your appropriate Brain States.

THE POWER OF SUPER HABITS

You might expect we'd start by directly tackling these foundational areas—fixing your sleep, changing your diet, establishing an exercise routine. But Sarah discovered something counterintuitive: the fastest way to improve these foundational habits is to first master what we call 'Super Habits.'

The 'Daily 3:1 Reflection' you learned in Chapter 1 is a good example of a Super Habit because it helps you to both plan and reflect. Super Habits work by helping Will Power guide HUE toward better patterns across all foundational areas simultaneously. Think of them as master keys that unlock multiple doors at once. The FAM Story is also a Super Habit, and you'll learn others in the coming chapters.

"This was a breakthrough moment for me," Sarah explained. "I kept trying to fix everything at once—my sleep, my diet, my exercise routine. But the Task Director showed me how consistently using the 3:1 Reflection actually made improving these other areas easier. Instead of fighting multiple battles, I was creating positive changes across my entire system."

Let's examine how the 3:1 Reflection naturally enhances each foundational area:

Sleep Enhancement: The evening reflection helps calm your thinking by redirecting HUE's spotlight away from threats and worries. This activation of your Recharge Brain State makes quality sleep more accessible. Sarah discovered that on nights when she skipped her reflection, her mind would race with unprocessed thoughts from the day.

Diet and Exercise Awareness: Regular reflection makes you more conscious of how your choices affect your energy and performance. When Sarah wrote about feeling energized after a morning walk or sluggish after a heavy lunch, these connections became clearer. This increased awareness naturally guided her toward better decisions without requiring constant willpower.

Stress Management: The practice of deliberately finding positives helps Will Power guide HUE toward calmer patterns. Each time you complete a reflection, you're training your brain to look beyond threats and problems. This builds your capacity to maintain balance even during challenging times.

Confidence Building: Writing down your daily successes, no matter how small, creates a more balanced view of your capabilities and progress. Many of us focus primarily on what went wrong or what's still incomplete. The 3:1 ratio ensures you're acknowledging more positives than areas for improvement.

Focus, Impact and Productivity Enhancement: Consistent reflection increases your awareness of which approaches work best, helping you match tasks to your optimal Brain States. Sarah began noticing patterns in her most focused days, which helped her design better schedules and routines.

"Understanding Super Habits was exceptionally insightful," Sarah shared. "Instead of feeling overwhelmed by all the areas I needed to improve, I could focus on one powerful practice that naturally enhanced everything else. The Task Director helped me see that mastering these key habits was like finding shortcuts to better Brain States across the board."

In the next chapter, you'll discover exactly where you stand on each foundational area and learn how to use Super Habits to strengthen your base for optimal performance.

18

MEASURING AND STRENGTHENING YOUR FOUNDATION

Success Cycle location: Step 2; Progress: 80% complete

N ow that you understand how Super Habits like the 3:1 Reflection can enhance your foundational areas, let's measure your current patterns. To identify which areas need your attention, take *The Human-AI Readiness Brain State Assessment* again (on the next page). This time, rather than focusing on your overall score, pay attention to the areas where you score highest—these indicate which habits need the most work.

Think of this assessment like running a diagnostic check on your foundational habits. Each statement reveals something important about how your brain is functioning across the foundational areas we discussed. Take a moment to rate yourself honestly on each statement below, scoring from 1 (never) to 10 (always).

Write down your score for each statement.

Here are the statements:

1. I find myself responding to urgent issues instead of having a plan (or sticking to my plan). *Score:* _____

    Notes: _____

2. I get interrupted (by others, emails/phone, and my own self-doubt/ negative self-talk) and it takes me longer to complete my work.

    Score: _____

    Notes: _____

3. I sleep poorly and it takes longer to complete my work to a high standard. *Score:* _____

    Notes: _____

4. I waste time doubting my decisions, second-guessing myself, and beating myself up. *Score:* _____

    Notes: _____

5. My mind feels foggy and it slows down my work. *Score:* _____

    Notes: _____

6. I put off important tasks even though I know they need doing.

    Score: _____

    Notes: _____

7. I feel overwhelmed and I make mistakes that take time to fix (meaning it takes longer to complete my work to a high standard).

    Score: _____

    Notes: _____

8. I find myself scrolling social media when I know it is not a good use of my time/helpful for me being at my best. *Score:* _____

    Notes: _____

9. I sleep poorly and it makes it harder to spot and prevent mistakes in my work. *Score:* _____

    Notes: _____

10. My mind jumps between tasks instead of focusing on one thing (meaning it takes me longer to complete my work). *Score:* _____

   Notes: _____

11. I get distracted (including by my own self-doubt/negative self-talk) meaning it takes longer to complete my work to a high standard.

   Score: _____

   Notes: _____

12. I feel like I could achieve more if I felt more confident and focused.

   Score: _____

   Notes: _____

13. I waste time because I'm not thinking clearly. *Score:* _____

   Notes: _____

14. My diet choices leave me feeling sluggish and it takes me longer to complete my work to a high standard. *Score:* _____

   Notes: _____

15. Lack of regular exercise for example, ten thousand plus steps and elevated heart rate, reduces my mental energy and focus. *Score:* _____

   Notes: _____

Please note: You can access a digital version of this self-assessment which shows you an overview of your scores at: tougherminds.co.uk/trainyourbrain

UNDERSTANDING YOUR RESULTS

After completing the assessment, you might feel overwhelmed by all the areas that need attention. This is exactly how Sarah felt at first. "Looking at my scores was daunting," she shared. "But the Task Director helped me see something important: I didn't need to fix everything at once. By focusing on consistently using the 3:1 Reflection, I started seeing improvements across multiple areas."

This is why we start with Super Habits. Consider what happened when Sarah established a consistent evening 3:1 Reflection practice:

First Week:
- She began noticing patterns in her sleep quality
- Writing down positives helped calm her racing mind
- The practice itself became a signal to her brain that the workday was ending

Second Week:
- She started recognizing how different foods affected her energy
- The impact of her exercise patterns became more apparent in her daily reflections
- She could see clear connections between stress and productivity

Third Week:
- Her confidence grew as she documented small wins
- Sleep improved as evening reflection became routine
- Other positive habits started feeling more natural

CREATING YOUR FOUNDATION

Based on your assessment results, choose just one or two specific habits to focus on this week. Remember Sarah's experience—start with mastering the 3:1 Reflection, then let other improvements follow naturally. Take a moment to identify:

1. Which foundational area needs the most attention this month?
2. How could consistent use of the 3:1 Reflection help address this area?
3. What small step will you take today to establish your reflection practice?

The Task Director has a saying: "The foundation determines the height." Just as a lighthouse can't send its beam far without a solid base, you can't maintain optimal Brain States without strong foundational habits. But rather than trying to build everything at once, focus first on mastering the Super Habits that make all other improvements easier.

MOVING FORWARD

You might be wondering about specific strategies for better sleep, diet, exercise, stress management, confidence, focus, leadership, or other foundational practices. While these are crucial for your long-term success, diving into those details now would take us away from your most important immediate goal: mastering the Success Cycle itself.

Think of the Success Cycle as the ultimate Super Habit—the system that makes building all other habits easier. When you're ready to explore deeper insights into habit formation and Super Habits, you'll find comprehensive guidance in Appendix C. For additional insights about building specific habits at individual, team, and leadership levels, please see my best-selling book 'The Habit Mechanic' where I share over thirty habit building tools.

But for now, let's focus on completing Step 2 of the Success Cycle.

In the next chapter, you'll learn how to organize your tasks into clear priorities, creating the foundation the Day Designer will use to craft schedules that optimize your Brain States. As Sarah discovered, this simple but crucial step transforms how you use your energy each day.

19

ORGANIZING YOUR PRIORITY TASKS FOR THE NEXT 30 DAYS

Success Cycle location: Step 2; Progress: 90% complete

Let's build on what you've already accomplished with the Task Director. Through your FAM Story, you've connected your long-term vision to shorter-term goals. You've also identified key foundational habits that will help optimize your Brain States. Now it's time to get clear about all the tasks you need to complete.

Think about your daily tasks and responsibilities. They fall into two distinct categories based on the type of Brain State they require and we use the metaphor of ice to help us understand them and use them effectively:

Ice Cubes are your routine tasks—the kind that need consistent but not maximum brain power. These tasks work well with your Medium Charge Brain State. Think of routine emails, basic admin work, or standard meetings.

Many of these tasks can be automated or semi-automated with AI tools.

Figure 19.1: Think of doing your busy work like freezing ice cubes.

Ice Sculptures are your complex tasks—the ones that demand sustained premium thinking. These require your High Charge Brain State. This includes not only challenging work projects like strategic planning or creative development but also the focused effort needed to build those foundational habits you identified earlier. Increasingly these tasks can be made easier with AI tools.

Figure 19.2: Think of doing your focused, creative, and problem-solving work like building ice sculptures.

"The Task Director helped me see this distinction clearly," Sarah shared. "Writing my novel was definitely an ice sculpture—it needed my best thinking energy, but I could also use next-generation AI to help me write faster. However, processing team updates was more like freezing ice cubes—something I could handle in Medium Charge state or even delegate to AI tools. Understanding this difference helped me stop wasting my High Charge hours on tasks that didn't really need them."

CREATING YOUR ORGANIZED TASK LISTS

Follow these steps to create your organized task lists:

1. First, write down everything you need to accomplish in the **next 30 days** that isn't part of your normal day-to-day routine. Include work, family responsibilities, personal development tasks and anything else you think is relevant. Don't worry about categorizing yet—just get a complete brain dump onto paper.

3. Label each task as either an "ice cube" or "ice sculpture."

4. For each ice sculpture task:

- Assign a priority number (1 being your highest priority)
- Estimate how many minutes or hours it will likely take to complete

5. For each ice cube task:

- Assign a priority number (1 being highest priority)
- Estimate how many minutes or hours it will likely take to complete

Here's how Sarah's lists looked:

Ice Sculptures (High Charge Tasks):

- Continue to build my Daily 3:1 Reflection habit (Priority 1, 3 minutes per day)
- Develop new customer service strategy (Priority 3, 12 hours)
- Establish morning exercise routine (Priority 2, 20 minutes per day)
- Learn new AI data analysis system (Priority 4, 8 hours)
- Write first novel chapter (Priority 5, 15 hours)

- Decorate the kitchen (Priority 6, 20 hours)

Ice Cubes (Medium Charge Tasks):
- Review daily team reports (Priority 5, 1 hour)
- Update project trackers (Priority 2, 30 minutes)
- Schedule recurring meetings (Priority 3, 30 mins)
- Call Sam to provide project update (Priority 1, 30 mins)
- Renew my passport (Priority 5, 1 hour)

"Creating these structured lists gave me a completely new perspective," Sarah explained. "Instead of just reacting to whatever seemed urgent, I could be strategic about using my Brain States. The Task Director helped me see exactly when I needed my High Charge hours and plan accordingly."

THREE ESSENTIAL MAINTENANCE STRATEGIES

The Task Director showed Sarah three important strategies for maintaining this system:

1. Schedule Weekly Reviews

Every Sunday evening, Sarah would update her lists with new tasks and review existing ones. "Sometimes tasks I thought would be ice sculptures actually became more like ice cubes as I got better at them," she explained. "For example, once I learned the new AI data analysis system, using it became a Medium Charge task. Other times, what I thought would be a simple ice cube turned out to need more focused thinking."

2. Create a Task Inbox System

Sarah kept a "task inbox"—a single place to capture new responsibilities as they came up. "Every evening, I'd review this inbox," she shared. "I categorize each new task as either an ice cube or sculpture, assign it a priority, estimate the time needed, and added it to the appropriate list. This prevented new tasks from disrupting my Brain State optimization."

3. Review Time Estimates Regularly

"I learned to track how long it actually took me to complete ice sculpture tasks versus my initial estimates," Sarah explained. "This helped me become more accurate in my planning." I also discovered something interesting about timing, Sarah explained. "Tasks often took different amounts of time based on my Brain State. A report that might take three hours when I was foggy could be finished in 45 minutes during High Charge times. Understanding these patterns helped me create much more realistic schedules with the Day Designer."

Take time now to create your own prioritized lists.
If it's helpful, include the Success Cycle as one of your ice sculpture tasks.

Remember, nothing in this approach is prescriptive, so create your lists in the way that is most helpful for you.

Also, remember, this isn't just about work tasks, it's about everything that's important in your life.

CONGRATULATIONS! YOU'VE NOW COMPLETED STEP 2 OF THE SUCCESS CYCLE ☺

Before we move on, and if you think it's helpful, take a moment to think about people you admire for their ability to prioritize and plan effectively—whether it's a colleague, a leader you respect, or even a renowned business figure. What makes their approach so effective? This might help you to improve your relationship with your own Task Director. And you might even name it after one of those people you admire.

Next, we'll move onto Step 3, where you'll discover how the Day Designer uses these priority lists to craft schedules that optimize your Brain States across each 24-hour period. But first, organize your tasks clearly for the next 30 days. As Sarah discovered, this simple step creates the foundation for transforming how you use your energy each day.

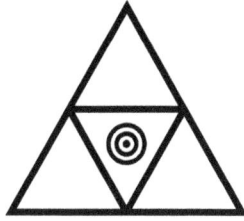

Success Cycle: Step 3

OPTIMIZATION WITH THE DAY DESIGNER

"Planning transforms energy."

- Day Designer

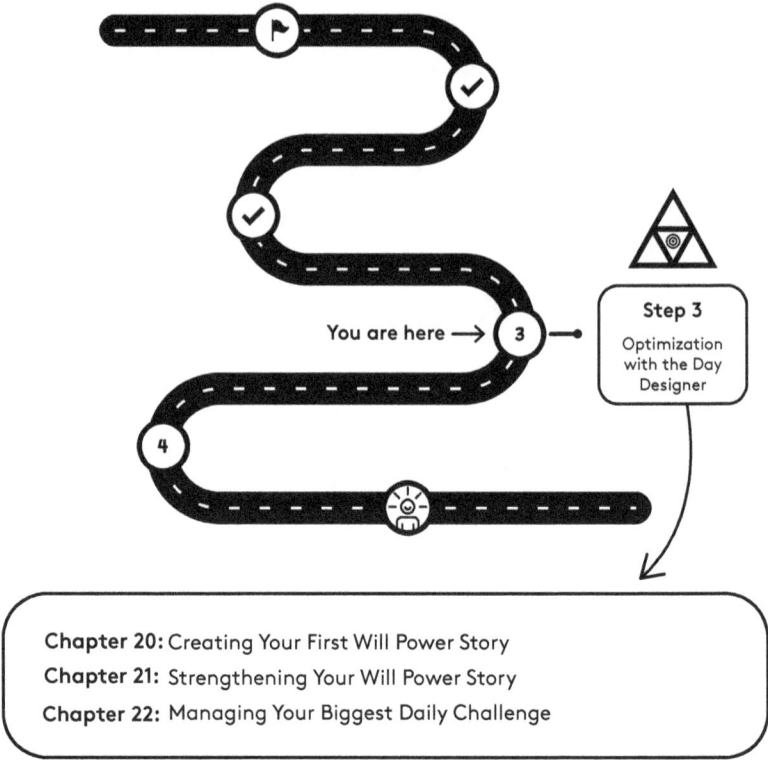

Step 3

Optimization with the Day Designer

You are here →

Chapter 20: Creating Your First Will Power Story
Chapter 21: Strengthening Your Will Power Story
Chapter 22: Managing Your Biggest Daily Challenge

Figure S3.1: An overview of your journey through Step 3.

20

CREATING YOUR FIRST
WILL POWER STORY

S arah looked down at her task lists, now neatly organized into ice sculptures and ice cubes. "I knew which tasks needed my best thinking," she
told me later, "but I still wasn't sure when to do them. That's when the Day
Designer introduced me to something that revolutionized my approach to
planning—the Will Power Story."

Think of your Will Power Story as a simple map that matches your tasks
to your brain's natural and enhanced energy patterns. Just as your FAM Story
guides your long-term journey, your Will Power Story helps you navigate
each day's steps along that path.

Today

Plan Your Day - create a Will Power Story

Use the timeline to plan out the commitments you have tomorrow or today. Then circle the activity or commitment that will be most challenging.

Plan when you will use Will Power Boosters and Strengths to help your day run smoothly:

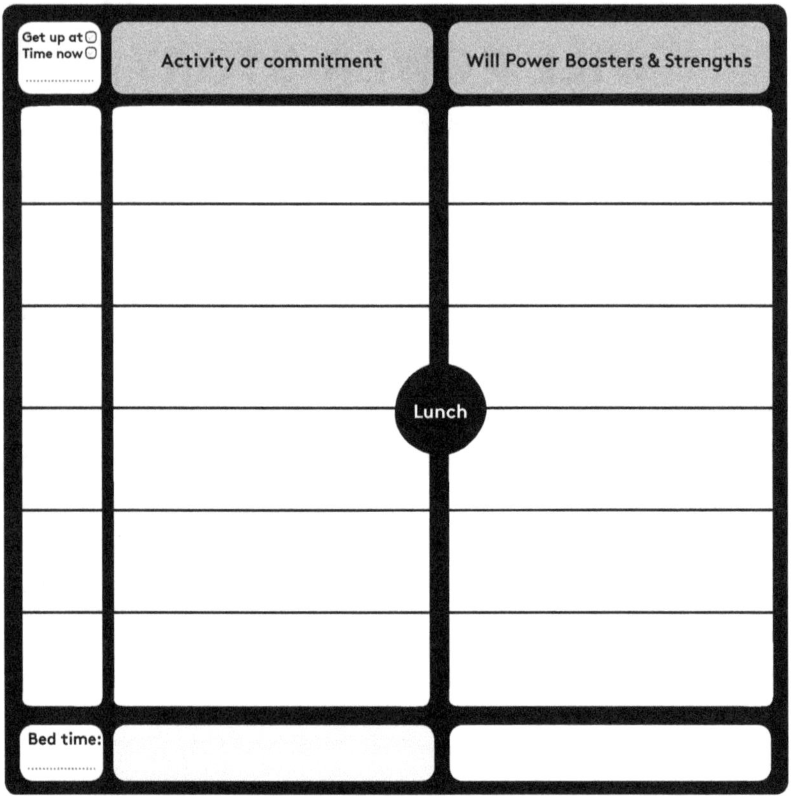

Get up at ○ Time now ○	Activity or commitment	Will Power Boosters & Strengths
	Lunch	
Bed time:		

Figure 20.1: A blank Will Power Story template.
You will understand each element by the end of chapter 22.

The Day Designer has a saying: "Planning transforms energy." Just as a lighthouse operator needs to understand weather patterns and deliberately manage their beam's power to maximize its reach across changing conditions, we need to actively plan how we use our Brain States rather than letting them operate randomly. Through deliberate planning, we can transform our basic energy patterns into optimized states—whether through our own management practices or strategic AI use—reaching levels of performance that wouldn't be possible through natural patterns alone. This is why planning isn't just about organizing tasks—it's about understanding and deliberately shaping the energy we bring to those tasks.

"What made this tool so powerful," Sarah explained, "was how it showed me when to use my brain's High Charge state for important work, and when to handle routine tasks in Medium Charge states. Instead of fighting my energy patterns, I could work with them."

LEVERAGING YOUR AI SUPPORT SYSTEM

"When I first categorized my tasks," Sarah shared, "I realized something important about my AI tools. Some could handle my ice cube tasks almost entirely, like summarizing routine meetings or drafting basic emails. Others could enhance my ice sculpture work - not by replacing my thinking, but by handling supporting tasks while I focused on innovation."

Consider your own tasks in two categories:

1. Ice cubes that AI could handle (e.g., routine emails, basic research, standard reports)
2. Ice sculptures where AI could support and augment your premium thinking (e.g., strategic planning, creative work, complex problem-solving)

Don't worry if you're not sure exactly how AI can support different types of tasks. The key thing is to start thinking about this and to begin considering how you might use these tools more strategically throughout your day. Remember, you don't need to figure it all out at once—this understanding will develop naturally as you work with your Will Power Story. For now, let's focus on creating that story.

CREATING YOUR FIRST WILL POWER STORY

You'll need:

- A blank piece of paper
- Your ice sculpture and ice cube lists from the previous chapter
- 15 minutes of quiet time

Step 1: Draw Your Basic Timeline

Turn your paper sideways (landscape) and draw a horizontal line across the middle (from one end of the page to the other). Now, divide this line into eight key parts of your day:

- Wake up
- Early morning
- Mid-morning
- Lunch time
- Early afternoon
- Late afternoon
- Evening
- Bedtime

"Just seeing my day laid out like this," Sarah shared, "helped me be more realistic about what I could accomplish."

Step 2: Mark Your High Charge Times

Most people have their best thinking energy in the morning, but this varies. On your timeline, mark when you typically:

- Feel most alert and focused (High Charge)
- Have less mental energy (Medium Charge)

Sarah discovered something important: "I realized I'm sharpest from 8 AM to 11 AM, then have another good period from 3 PM to 5 PM. This became the foundation for planning my day."

Step 3: Place Your Ice Sculpture Tasks

Match your ice sculpture tasks to your High Charge times. Here are some examples:

- Complete complex planning during morning High Charge peak
- Have important meetings when you are most alert
- Do your creative work during afternoon High Charge time

Step 4: Fill in Routine Tasks

Place your ice cube tasks during:

- Natural energy dips
- Between demanding tasks
- When you know you'll have less focus

Here's an example to help you pull everything together:

Time	Type of Work
6:00 AM	Wake up
7:00 AM	Start my day
8:00 AM	Ice sculpture (High Charge)
10:00 AM	Ice sculpture (High Charge)
12:00 PM	Break
1:00 PM	Ice cubes (Medium Charge)
3:00 PM	Ice sculpture (High Charge)
5:00 PM	Ice cubes (Medium Charge)
5:30 PM	Wind down (e.g., complete a Daily 3:1 Reflection)
9:30 PM	Bedtime

START SMALL

"I started by just planning my morning hours," Sarah recalled. "Once that worked, I gradually expanded to the full day. The key was keeping it simple at first." She smiled as she remembered how this approach paid off: "Once I expanded to evening planning, I discovered something powerful. Including my 3:1 Reflection in my Will Power Story helped both habits grow stronger—good planning supported better reflection, and better reflection led to clearer planning."

COMMON CHALLENGES TO WATCH FOR

1. **Trying to Do Too Much:** "I learned the hard way," Sarah shared, "that you can only do about 4-5 hours of premium thinking work each day—and sometimes over 6 hours when you get the AI working with you. Trying to do more just doesn't work."

2. **Fighting Your Patterns:** Don't schedule demanding work when your brain naturally needs rest. Move ice sculptures to your High Charge times.

YOUR NEXT STEPS

1. Create tomorrow's basic Will Power Story:

- Draw your timeline
- Mark your typical High Charge times
- Place just 1-3 ice sculptures to work on during these times
- Fill in some ice cubes around them

2. Notice what works:

- When did you feel most focused?
- Which times worked best for important tasks?
- When was routine work easier?

Remember, this is just your first attempt. Keep it simple, be patient, and let the Day Designer guide you toward your optimal rhythm. The key is getting started with something you can actually use tomorrow.

21

STRENGTHENING YOUR WILL POWER STORY

Success Cycle location: Step 3; Progress: 50% complete

S arah had been using her basic Will Power Story for a week, matching her ice sculptures to her High Charge times. "I was getting better results," she told me later, "but sometimes I still struggled to maintain those High Charge states. That's when the Day Designer showed me how to protect and strengthen my best thinking hours."

This is where two powerful resources come into play—your Strengths and Will Power Boosters. Think of these as the support systems that help you maintain your optimal Brain States, especially during important High Charge work.

"These resources supercharged how I approached each day," Sarah explained. "Instead of just hoping I'd stay focused during important work, I had specific strategies to protect my thinking time."

YOUR LIGHTHOUSE BRAIN'S SUPPORT SYSTEM

Remember how your Lighthouse Brain needs different power states throughout the day. Just as a lighthouse needs systems to maintain its beam at full power, your brain needs support to maintain its High Charge state. This is especially crucial when working on your ice sculptures—those tasks that require your premium thinking power.

UNDERSTANDING YOUR STRENGTHS

Strengths are your natural abilities for maintaining focused states. Key ones include:

- **Self-controlled:** You stay focused on priorities and avoid distractions
- **Persistent:** You motivate yourself to keep going when things get tough
- **Perspective:** You step back from the immediate to reflect and plan
- **Efficient:** You organize well and minimize wasted effort
- **Optimistic:** You stay positive when things don't go to plan

Strengths

Self-controlled
You stay focused on your priorities and avoid distractions.

Persistent
You motivate yourself to keep going even when things are tough.

Perspective
You step-back from the here-and-now to reflect and plan.

Efficient
You are organized & do things with little wasted effort.

Leading
You help others to get the best out of themselves.

Empathic
You understand how your colleagues, family, and friends are feeling when they are having a tough time.

Optimistic
You stay hopeful and positive even when things are not going to plan.

Figure 21.1: Use your Strengths to improve your focus and productivity.

"Learning about these Strengths was enlightening," Sarah shared. "I realized I was naturally good at being Persistent, but needed to work on being Self-controlled. This helped me know exactly what to focus on."

ADDING WILL POWER BOOSTERS

While Strengths are your internal capabilities, Will Power Boosters are specific actions that protect your Brain States.

Key boosters include:

- **Phone management:** Turn off your phone to minimize distractions
- **Internet management:** Disconnect to reduce quick-check temptations
- **Workspace plan:** Create an environment with minimal distractions
- **Concentration booster:** Write down a focus plan before starting

Will Power Boosters

Confidence booster
Do not beat yourself up if you make a mistake, keep trying.

Phone management
Turn off your phone to minimize distractions & get more done.

Mindset
Approach tasks & activities on time & in the right frame of mind.

Internet management
Disconnect the internet to reduce the temptation of quickly checking your emails, or favorite website.

Concentration booster
At the start of a challenging task or job, write down a concentration plan to help you focus.

Activation booster
Exercise at lunch or break to boost Activation e.g., a 10-minute walking break.

Workspace plan
Create a workspace with minimal distractions.

Concentration control
Use Focus Words and Pictures to control concentration.

Figure 21.2: Use Will Power Boosters to improve your focus and productivity.

STRATEGIC AI MANAGEMENT

Sarah discovered that AI tools could either boost or drain her Brain States. "Just like my phone, I learned to manage AI tools strategically," she explained. "During High Charge periods, I'd use them to enhance my thinking—having them analyze data while I focused on strategy. During Medium Charge periods, they could handle routine tasks."

Examples of how you could use AI during High Charge periods to outsource brain power:

- Use AI to support and augment complex thinking
- Have AI handle background research while you experiment and innovate
- Let AI explore alternatives while you focus on strategic decisions

Examples of how you could use AI during Medium Charge periods:

- Let AI handle routine communications
- Use AI for standard information processing
- Automate repetitive tasks completely

ENHANCING YOUR WILL POWER STORY

Here's an example of how you can enhance your basic Will Power Story with Strengthens and Will Power Boosters:

Time	Activity	Brain State	Strengths	Boosters
8:00 AM	Strategic work (ice sculpture)	High Charge	Self-controlled	Phone off, quiet space
10:00 AM	Team meeting	High Charge	Leading	Meeting plan ready
1:00 PM	Routine tasks	Medium Charge	Efficient	-
3:00 PM	Creative work	High Charge	Persistent	Internet off

To make it easier to create a complete Will Power Story, I have created a PDF template. Go to <u>tougherminds.co.uk/trainyourbrain</u> to download your copy.

START SIMPLE

Begin by adding just one or two Strengths and Boosters to your most important High Charge period. "I started with just my morning planning time," Sarah explained. "Once that worked well, I gradually added support to other parts of my day."

COMMON CHALLENGES

1. **Using Too Many Boosters:** Start with just the essential ones. Sarah found this out: "At first I tried using every booster. It was overwhelming. Starting with just phone management made it much easier."
2. **Forgetting To Use Your Strengths:** Make a note of which Strengths help most during High Charge work. Build on these natural capabilities.

YOUR NEXT STEPS

1. Identify your key Strengths:

- Which ones do you naturally use well?
- Which could help with your High Charge work?

2. Choose your essential Boosters:

- What most often interrupts your focus?
- Which Boosters would help most?

3. Update tomorrow's Will Power Story:

- Add 1-2 Strengths to your main High Charge period
- Include one key Will Power Booster

Remember, start small with just one or two supports. The goal isn't to use every Strength and Will Power Booster at once, but to gradually build a system that helps you maintain your best thinking states when they matter most.

22

MANAGING YOUR BIGGEST
DAILY CHALLENGE

Success Cycle location: Step 3; Progress: 75% complete

S arah had been using her Will Power Story for two weeks, matching tasks
to Brain States and using Strengths and Will Power Boosters. "While I
was making progress," she reflected, "there was still one persistent challenge
in my daily routine—that post-lunch energy crash.

That's when the Day Designer showed me how to use the SWAP to over-
come my biggest daily challenge."

Most people have one part of their day that consistently causes problems.
For many, like Sarah, it's post-lunch. For others, it might be early mornings,
late afternoons, or switching off in the evening. The SWAP helps you tackle
this challenge systematically.

"What made SWAP so powerful," Sarah explained, "was how it helped me
turn the most challenging part of my day into a genuine Recharge opportunity. Instead of fighting my energy dip, I learned to work with it."

UNDERSTANDING SWAP

SWAP stands for:

- **Self-Watch:** Notice what's happening
- **Aim:** Choose a specific goal
- **Plan:** Create clear steps to achieve it

Let's see how Sarah used this to transform her challenging post-lunch dip in energy levels.

STEP 1: Self-Watch

First, Sarah observed exactly what happened after lunch:

- Felt mentally foggy
- Struggled to focus on work
- Often made mistakes
- Ended up scrolling on her phone

"Just paying attention helped me see the pattern," Sarah shared. "I was trying to do High Charge work when my brain was only capable of working on Medium Charge tasks."

STEP 2: Aim

Next, Sarah set a clear, specific goal: "Complete my list of afternoon ice cube tasks effectively despite the energy dip."

Notice how this Aim is:

- Specific (focused on a clear list of afternoon work)
- States a positive action (complete a list of tasks)
- Measurable (the tasks will either be completed or not)

STEP 3: Plan

Finally, Sarah created a simple plan to support her Aim—which included strategic AI use:

- Light lunch to avoid feeling 'heavy' and experience indigestion
- 15-minute walk to refresh energy
- Clear list of afternoon ice cube tasks
- Used AI to help her draft replies to urgent emails.
- Used Self-control to turn off her phone to minimize distractions.

"Having a specific plan was very powerful," Sarah explained. "Instead of just hoping I'd somehow push through, I had clear steps to follow."

STRATEGIC AI MANAGEMENT

"I realized AI could help manage the most challenging part of my day," Sarah explained. "Instead of forcing myself to do complex work when my energy dipped, I could use AI to help me write some draft emails I needed to reply to whilst I recovered."

ADDING A SWAP TO YOUR WILL POWER STORY

Look at your Will Power Story and circle the most challenging part of your day—when it's most difficult to get into the Brain State you need to be at your best. This might be:

- When you struggle most with focus
- A time you often waste
- When you feel least productive

- When you worry and beat yourself up a lot
- When you have trouble transitioning from work to rest in the evening

Now create your SWAP (use's Sarah's example for inspiration):

1. Self-Watch: What exactly happens during this time?

_____

2. Aim: What specific outcome do you want instead?

_____

3. Plan: What 2-3 part plan will you create to help you achieve the specific outcome you want?

_____

_____

_____

Start Simple Begin with just one small change. "I started with just the lunchtime walk," Sarah explained. "Once that became natural, I added the other elements. Small steps made it sustainable."

COMMON CHALLENGES

1. **Trying to Fight Your Pattern:** Don't try to schedule ice sculptures during the most challenging part of your day. Work with your brain's natural rhythms instead.
2. **Making the Plan Too Complex:** Keep your SWAP steps simple and specific. Sarah found this crucial: "The simpler my plan, the more likely I was to follow it."

YOUR NEXT STEPS

1. Identify your daily challenge:

- Circle it on your Will Power Story
- Notice exactly what happens
- Be specific about the timeframe

2. Create your simple SWAP:

- Self-Watch the pattern
- Set one clear Aim
- Make a 2-3 step Plan

3. Try it tomorrow:

- Focus on just one small change
- Notice what works
- Adjust as needed

The complete Will Power Story has three elements working together:

1. Basic timeline matching tasks to Brain States
2. Strengths and Will Power Boosters for support
3. SWAP for your biggest challenge

As Sarah discovered, this combination takes how you think about managing your day to new levels: "Once I had all three parts working together—matching tasks to energy, using the right support tools, and managing the most challenging parts of my day—everything became easier. I wasn't fighting my brain anymore; I was working with it."

But even with these tools mastered, Sarah faced one final challenge—making this new approach automatic rather than effortful. That's where Step 4 of the Success Cycle pulls everything together.

Plan Your Day - create a Will Power Story

i) Use the timeline to plan out the commitments you have tomorrow or today. Then circle the activity or commitment that will be most challenging.

Plan when you will use Will Power Boosters and Strengths to help your day run smoothly:

Get up at ☑ Time now ○ 6am	Activity or commitment	Will Power Boosters & Strengths
6.15am 7.15am 8am	- 25 minute run - increase Activation - DES SWAP - Travel to work.	- Self-controlled
8.30am - 10am	- Write a proposal for a new client - Graze (have a piece of fruit)	- Internet Management
10.30am - 1pm	- Run lunchtime webinar for investment bank client - 12 noon start	
1.30pm - 2.30pm	- Lunch [If I eat too much I will procrastinate in the afternoon!] - 15 minute walk	- Self-controlled
3pm - 5pm	- Reply to emails - Call Andrew - Plan tomorrow - Will Power Story - End of day written reflection	- Phone management - Workspace plan - Concentration control
5.30pm - 9pm	- Travel home - Food shopping, eat with family, relax with family	
Bed time: 10pm	- Get ready for bed - Reading in bed by 9:30pm	- Phone management

Lunch

ii) Why not create a small specific SWAP to help you manage the most challenging part of your day, which you have circled, more effectively?

☑ I need a SWAP   ☒ I feel strong, no SWAP needed

◎ Aim:	⚠ Plan:	⚠ Plan:	⚠ Plan:
Finish my afternoon to-do list after lunch.	Graze throughout the morning e.g. piece of fruit.	Light lunch. Post-lunch exercise - 15 mins walk.	Have a clear plan of work after lunch.

Figure 22.1: An example of a complete Will Power Story.

CONGRATULATIONS!
YOU'VE NOW COMPLETED STEP 3
OF THE SUCCESS CYCLE ☺

Before we move on, and if you think it's helpful, take a moment to think about people you admire for their ability to structure their day and manage their energy—whether it's a colleague, a mentor, or even a high-performing athlete. What makes their approach so effective? This might help you to improve your relationship with your own Day Designer. And you might even name it after one of those people you admire.

Next, we'll move onto Step 4, where you'll discover how to use behavioral science to make completing your daily Will Power Story automatic.

Success Cycle: Step 4

AUTOMATION WITH THE ROUTINE ENGINEER

"Systems beat struggle."

- Routine Engineer

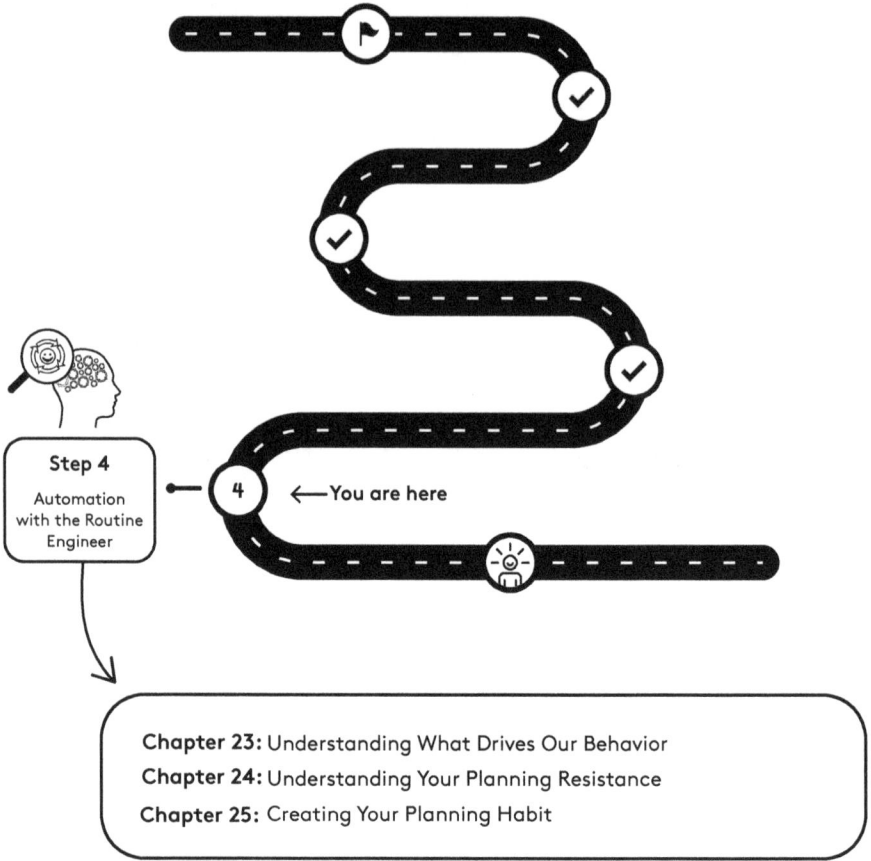

Step 4

Automation
with the Routine
Engineer

4   ←—You are here

Chapter 23: Understanding What Drives Our Behavior
Chapter 24: Understanding Your Planning Resistance
Chapter 25: Creating Your Planning Habit

Figure S4.1: An overview of your journey through Step 4.

23

UNDERSTANDING WHAT DRIVES OUR BEHAVIOR

N ow that you've learned how to create your Will Power Story with the Day Designer, let's work with the Routine Engineer to make this powerful tool automatic. Just as Sarah discovered, knowing what to do is only the first step—the real transformation comes from turning that knowledge into lasting habits.

"The Will Power Story proved invaluable whenever I implemented it," Sarah admitted. "Though initially, I struggled to make it a consistent practice, or I'd make excuses about being too busy. The Routine Engineer helped me understand exactly why this happened and how to change it."

The Routine Engineer has a saying that captures this perfectly: "Systems beat struggle."

This is where our proprietary 9 Action Factor Habit Mechanic System transforms everything. While other approaches focus on just one or two aspects of habit formation, this comprehensive system integrates all the essential elements that behavioral science shows matter for lasting change. Let's explore these nine factors that make sustainable change possible, using the Will Power Story planning habit as an example:

THE NINE FACTORS FOR
BUILDING YOUR PLANNING HABIT

1. **Habit Mechanic Mindset**—believing change is possible "Initially, I doubted I could maintain a daily planning habit," Sarah shared. "But the Routine Engineer helped me see evidence that my brain could build new patterns. Just as I'd learned to automatically check my phone, I could learn to automatically plan my day."

**Habit Mechanic
Mindset**

*Figure 23.1: If you don't believe you can improve, you never will.
The right mindset is essential for changing your habits.*

2. **Brain State Optimization**—having the right energy for change Sarah discovered a two-step approach that transformed her planning: "At first, I tried creating my Will Power Story when I was tired at day's end. It never worked. Then I discovered a better way—a quick update of my task list at the end of the day, followed by creating my actual Will Power Story first thing in the morning. With good sleep and morning exercise charging up my brain, planning became almost effortless."

Brain State

Figure 23.2: To successfully build new habits,
your brain needs to be neurobiologically ready for change.

3. **Tiny Change Factor**—starting small enough to succeed Rather than attempting a complete Will Power Story immediately, Sarah began with just planning her morning hours. Small successes built momentum for bigger changes.

Tiny Changes

Figure 23.3: You can change but only one tiny step at a time.

4. **Personal Motivation**—connecting to meaningful goals "The Routine Engineer helped me see how daily planning directly supported my FAM Story goals," Sarah explained. "Better planning meant better

Brain States, which meant more energy for being my best at work, being present with family, and even finding time to work on my novel."

**Personal
Motivation**

Figure 23.4: It is easier to change if there is a meaningful reason why.

5. Personal Knowledge and Skills—understanding what to do
Through working with the Day Designer, Sarah had learned how to create an effective Will Power Story. This knowledge was essential for building the habit.

**Personal Knowledge
& Skills**

Figure 23.5: Building new habits often requires you to learn new things.

6. Community Knowledge and Skills—learning from others Sarah began sharing Will Power Story techniques with her team, which deepened her own understanding and commitment to the practice.

**Community
Knowledge & Skills**

Figure 23.6: If the people around you already know how to do the thing you want to learn (e.g., create a Will Power Story), it will be easier for you to learn it.

7. Social Influence—getting support from others and being a good role model for others "When my team started creating their own Will Power Stories, it made it easier for me to maintain mine and vice versa," Sarah shared. "We'd check in about our plans and share what worked."

Social Influence

Figure 23.7: If the people around you are already doing the thing you want to do, it will be easier for you to do it.

8. Rewards and Penalties—seeing clear consequences Sarah discovered three types of rewards from daily planning:

- Intrinsic (feeling more in control)
- Extrinsic (getting more done)
- Social (inspiring her team)

Rewards & Penalties

Figure 23.8: Rewards encourage behavior and penalties discourage it.

9. External Triggers—creating helpful reminders Sarah set up specific cues for both phases of her planning: "I scheduled two short meetings with myself—a 10-minute review at day's end to list tomorrow's tasks, and a 10-minute planning session first thing in the morning to create my Will Power Story. Having these as actual calendar appointments made them feel as important as any other meeting."

Physical & Digital Environment

Figure 23.9: It is easier to do things if you get triggered (reminded) to do them.

MAKING THESE FACTORS WORK TOGETHER

Understanding these factors isn't enough—you need to get them working together in harmony. Think about how your smartphone activates these factors:

- It's always within reach (External Triggers)
- It promises immediate benefits (Rewards)
- It creates social connection (Social Influence)
- It's easy to use (Personal Knowledge and Skills)
- It starts with simple actions (Tiny Changes)

Your Will Power Story habit needs a similar approach. That's why the Routine Engineer helps you create a complete Habit Building Plan that activates all nine factors together.

REFLECT ON YOUR OWN HABIT BUILDING

To get you thinking about your Will Power Story habit and the nine factors, consider these questions:

- Do you truly believe you can build this habit? (Habit Mechanic Mindset)
- When does your brain have the right energy for planning? (Brain State)
- What tiny first step could you take? (Tiny Change Factor)
- How does daily planning connect to your deeper goals? (Personal Motivation)
- What reminders could you set up? (External Triggers)

If you're curious about the scientific principles behind the 9 Action Factor behavior change model and how it relates to optimizing Brain States in the AI era, you'll find this detailed explanation in Appendix D. However, let's stay focused on our immediate goal: working with your Routine Engineer to make Brain State optimization automatic.

In the next chapter, you'll learn exactly how to create this integrated Habit Building Plan. Remember, the Routine Engineer's goal isn't just to help you use the Will Power Story occasionally—it's to make this powerful tool as automatic as checking your phone. When daily planning becomes a habit, you create a foundation for optimizing all your Brain States.

24

UNDERSTANDING YOUR PLANNING RESISTANCE

Success Cycle location: Step 4; Progress: 50% complete

Sarah focused on her Will Power Story template, understanding the nine factors that could drive her planning habit but feeling uncertain about how to bring them all together. "The Routine Engineer helped me grasp an essential principle," she reflected. "Success isn't about tackling each factor separately—it's about creating a unified plan that makes them all work together."

Think of the Habit Building Plan like an architect's blueprint for your new habit. Just as a blueprint ensures all systems in a building work together—from foundation to roof—your Habit Building Plan coordinates all nine factors that drive behavior change.

"At first, I tried to force myself to plan through willpower alone," Sarah shared. "It was like trying to build a house with just a hammer. The Habit

141

Building Plan showed me how to create a complete system that would make planning feel natural rather than forced."

But before we can build this new habit, we need to understand what might stand in our way. Let's examine how your HUE (your Horribly, Unhelpful, Emotions) might resist this change.

UNDERSTANDING YOUR HUE'S RESISTANCE

Before creating your Habit Building Plan, consider which of these ways HUE typically resists planning. Mark whether you agree (✓) or disagree (✗):

How HUE Hinders Your Planning Habit

1. If planning doesn't immediately make my day better, it's not worth the effort. ☐
2. Responding to issues as they arise feels more productive than following a plan. ☐
3. It's better to just start working than spend time planning. ☐
4. If I can't stick to my plan perfectly, I might as well not make one. ☐
5. Being spontaneous is better than being structured. ☐
6. Getting straight to work feels better than taking time to plan. ☐
7. My colleagues don't spend time planning, so I'll look unproductive if I do. ☐
8. If my first few attempts at planning don't work perfectly, I'll never be good at it. ☐
9. It's not my fault when my day gets derailed. ☐
10. People will judge me if they see me spending time on planning. ☐
11. Even though planning would help, it makes me look less capable. ☐

12. Admitting I need to plan better shows weakness. ☐
13. I can skip planning today because I'll definitely start tomorrow. ☐
14. If I try to plan and fail to follow through, I'm a failure. ☐
15. Everyone else works reactively, so why shouldn't I? ☐

REFLECTING ON YOUR RESISTANCE

Now complete this sentence: "My HUE could stop me from building a planning habit because..."

Sarah's reflection revealed something important: "I realized my HUE was telling me that 'real' professionals just handle whatever comes up. Planning felt like admitting I couldn't cope. Understanding this resistance was crucial for moving forward."

In the next chapter, you'll learn exactly how to create your Habit Building Plan. First, take a moment to honestly assess your own resistance patterns. As Sarah discovered, understanding what holds you back is the first step to moving forward.

25

CREATING YOUR
PLANNING HABIT

N ow that you understand your HUE's resistance patterns, let's create your first Habit Building Plan. This comprehensive approach addresses both conscious and unconscious aspects of behavior change, making your new planning habit feel natural rather than forced.

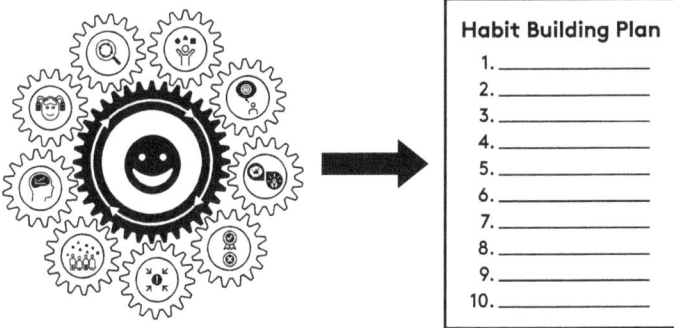

Habit Building Plan
1. _____
2. _____
3. _____
4. _____
5. _____
6. _____
7. _____
8. _____
9. _____
10. _____

Figure 25.1: The Habit Building Plan is designed to help you activate all Nine Action Factors.

CREATING YOUR FIRST HABIT BUILDING PLAN

To make it easier to create your first Habit Building Plan, I have created a PDF template. Go to tougherminds.co.uk/trainyourbrain to download your copy.

Now, work through each question carefully and write down your answers, being as specific as possible:

1. Describe the SMALL specific new helpful habit you want to build:

   Example answer: "Create my Will Power Story in my workbook at 8:30 AM at my desk in my 10-minute planning meeting with myself."

   Your answer: _____

2. Describe what you currently do instead:

   Example answer: "Jump straight into emails and urgent tasks without any plan, letting my inbox determine my priorities."

   Your answer: _____

3. Describe what triggers your current reactive pattern:

   Example answer: "Checking my phone first thing at my desk, seeing email notifications, and feeling pressure to respond immediately."

   Your answer: _____

4. Describe how you will remind yourself to create your Will Power Story:

   Example answer: "Schedule a daily 10-minute planning meeting at 8:30 AM in my calendar with automatic reminders."

   Your answer: _____

5. Describe the new knowledge and skills you need:

Example answer: "Understanding how to match different tasks to my Brain States and use my High Charge times effectively."

Your answer: _____

6. Where will you get this knowledge:

Example answer: "By creating daily Will Power Stories and review my progress using insights from this book."

Your answer: _____

7. Describe in detail WHY you want to build this planning habit:

Example answer: "To help me be at my best daily so I can capitalize on the opportunities emerging in the AI era and achieve my long-term FAM Story goals faster!"

Your answer: _____

8. Who can help you build this habit:

Example answer: "Share my daily Will Power Story with my team during our 9 AM stand-up meeting."

Your answer: _____

9. What will be your rewards:

Example answer: "Getting my most important work done by lunch, feeling clear and focused, having predictable energy for my family in the evenings, and having more time to work on my novel."

Your answer: _____

10. What will be the penalties for not building this habit:

Example answer: "Wasting my High Charge morning hours on routine tasks, feeling scattered and reactive, and having no energy left for what matters most."

Your answer: _____

SARAH'S SUCCESS STORY

"Creating this detailed plan revolutionized my approach," Sarah shared. "Instead of vague intentions about 'planning better,' I had a specific evening routine. Instead of fighting my HUE's resistance alone, I had support from my team. Most importantly, I could see exactly how planning connected to what mattered most—being my best at work, having energy for my novel, being present with family, and feeling in control of my day."

OVER TO YOU...

Take time now to complete your first 'Habit Building Plan' in as much detail as you can.

Remember, you're not just creating a plan; you're designing a new automatic pattern that will transform how you use your Brain States so you can thrive in the AI Era.

Before we move on, and if you think it's helpful, take a moment to think about people you admire for their ability to maintain consistent high performance—whether it's someone in your organization or a public figure known for sustainable excellence. What makes their approach so effective? This might help you to improve your relationship with your own Routine Engineer. And you might even name it after one of those people you admire.

CONGRATULATIONS! YOU'VE NOW COMPLETED YOUR FIRST LOOP OF THE SUCCESS CYCLE ☺

By working through all four steps—from understanding your current Brain State Score, to listing your ice cube and ice sculpture tasks with the Task Director, to optimizing your daily rhythm with the Day Designer, to making improvements automatic with the Routine Engineer—you've learned a systematic approach to mastering your Brain States in the AI era.

But this is only the beginning. To maintain and deepen your mastery:

1. Set yourself a challenge to create a Will Power Story daily for the next 5 days. Inside the Habit Mechanic University app, you'll see others doing the same.

Then in 30 days from now:

2. Review your FAM Story to see what progress you have made and retake the Human-AI Readiness Brain State Assessment

WHY 30 DAYS MATTERS

Through our work with thousands of professionals, we've discovered that 30 days is the optimal timeframe for seeing significant improvements in your Brain States. It's long enough to establish new patterns but short enough to maintain focused momentum. More importantly, it gives you a clear framework for implementing everything you've learned in this book.

The next 30 days could significantly improve how you work and live. Whether you're seeking promotion, starting or growing your business, building your team, or simply wanting more energy for what matters most, the tools you've learned can help you start creating the life you actually want to live—starting right now.

Remember, this isn't about achieving perfection in 30 days—it's about beginning a journey of continuous improvement through the Success Cycle. Each 30-day period becomes an opportunity to optimize your Brain States further and achieve significant goals in our AI-augmented world.

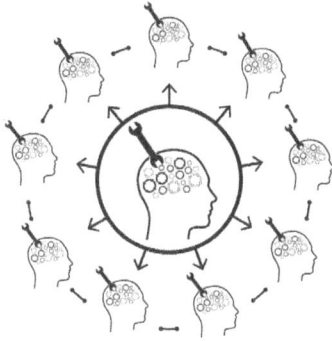

Step 5: Change Lives with the Success Cycle

COACHING & LEADING THE BRAIN STATE REVOLUTION

"In the AI Era, mastering our brains and Brain States will become humanity's most vital skill. But not many people know how! Will you join the mission to share this knowledge and help others transform their lives?"

- The Habit Mechanic

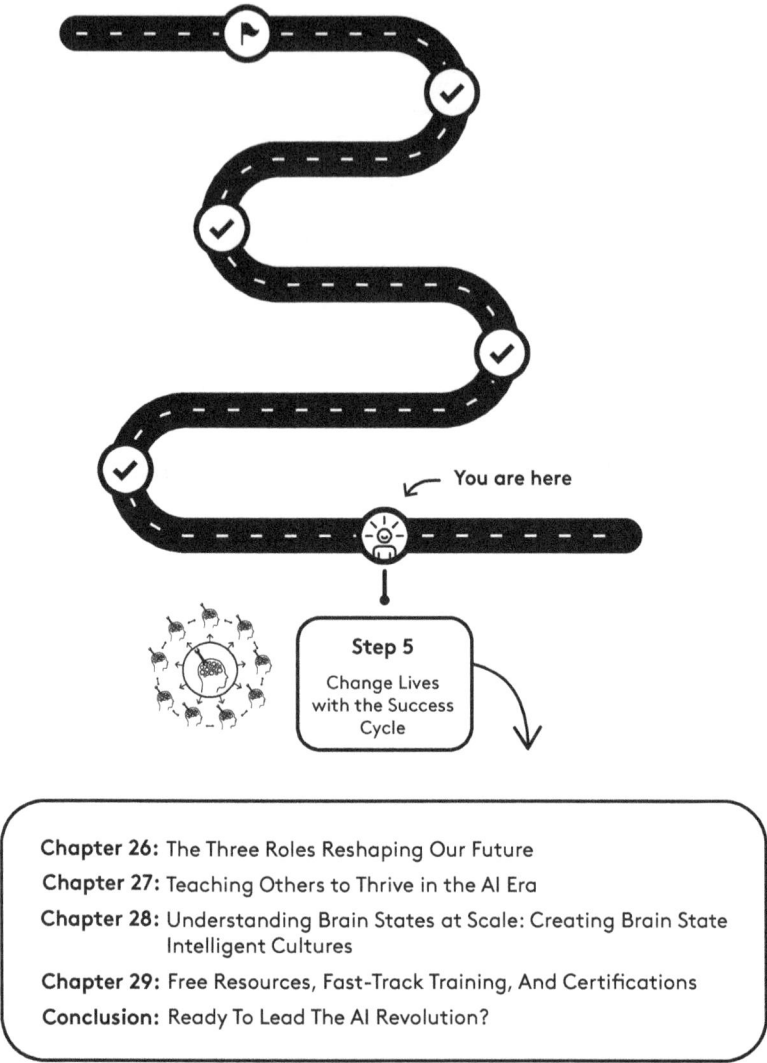

You are here

Step 5

Change Lives
with the Success
Cycle

Figure S5.1: Help others thrive in the AI Era.

HELP OTHERS
IN 60 SECONDS

Thank you for letting me guide you through the Success Cycle. I hope these tools for optimizing your Brain States have been valuable for you.

If you've found this approach helpful, would you take a moment to help others discover it?

Many people are struggling in our AI-augmented world—they want to be their best but lack the right tools and systems to make it happen.

In just 60 seconds, your honest review could help someone transform not just their work, but their entire life.

Here's how:

On Audible: Tap the three dots, select rate & review
On Kindle: Scroll to end, swipe up for review prompt
On other platforms: Visit the book's purchase page

Thank you for considering this.

Together, we can help others discover a better way to live and work in the AI era.

Dr. Jon Finn

26

THE THREE ROLES
RESHAPING OUR FUTURE

S arah sat at her desk, reflecting on how far she'd come in mastering her Brain States. "Something profound has shifted," she realized. "It's not just about using AI tools anymore—it's about understanding how humans and technology can truly enhance each other." This insight led her to a deeper revelation about the extraordinary transformation happening across every industry.

The AI revolution is transforming work in a fundamental way. The Industrial Revolution showed us how machines could take over physical labor, freeing humans from backbreaking manual work. Now, the AI Revolution is doing something similar with mental work—AI will handle most of the routine cognitive tasks humans are currently paid to do. This creates an extraordinary opportunity. Instead of spending our days on repetitive mental tasks, humans can focus on work that engages our unique cognitive abilities—the kind of thinking that's both more fulfilling for us and more valuable in the AI era.

Based on my deep understanding of human brain capabilities, potential limitations of AI technology, and my work with over 20,000 professionals,

I believe we're seeing the emergence of three distinct roles in this new era. While others might see different futures, I predict these roles will dominate how humans create value alongside AI. Here are the three distinct roles:

1. The Innovators
2. The Automators
3. The Human-AI Coaches

Here are more details on each:

1. THE INNOVATORS: CREATING OUR FUTURE

Innovators are literally creating the future before our eyes, using AI to extend their High Charge Brain States and human intelligence in ways previously unimaginable. Consider how medical researchers now use AI to screen millions of molecular combinations and identify promising antibiotic candidates in months instead of years—work that's crucial for fighting drug-resistant bacteria that threatens millions of lives worldwide.

These innovators are shaping our future by:

- Developing breakthrough vaccines and medical treatments
- Creating next-generation AI systems that transform industries
- Designing sustainable solutions for climate change
- Building new educational systems that personalize learning
- Revolutionizing healthcare delivery and patient care
- Transforming how we travel, live, and work
- Inventing new ways to produce and distribute clean energy

But here's what separates successful Innovators from those who struggle:

their Brain State profiles. The most effective Innovators maintain Arrowhead profiles (which I first introduced in chapter 9), consistently optimizing their daily premium cognitive performance. This difference enables them to:

- Direct AI tools with sustained clarity and focus
- Maintain creative energy for breakthrough thinking
- Innovate faster than competitors

2. THE AUTOMATORS: ENGINEERING THE FUTURE

The second role is already transforming how we live and work. Think about how banking has been transformed through automation. What once required visiting a physical branch, waiting in line, and interacting with tellers for every transaction now happens instantly through your smartphone. The modern banking experience demonstrates how Automators are revolutionizing traditional industries. But this is just the beginning.

Automators are creating two types of solutions:

Physical Automation:

- Advanced robotics for manufacturing and warehouses
- Automated delivery systems and autonomous vehicles
- Smart machinery for construction and agriculture
- Automated medical equipment and diagnostic tools
- Next-generation robots that handle dangerous tasks
- Intelligent production lines that adapt in real-time

Digital Automation:

- AI systems that handle routine office tasks
- Software that automates customer service and support
- Intelligent systems for data analysis and reporting
- Digital workflows that streamline business processes
- Platforms that automate financial planning
- Smart systems that optimize supply chains

Again, the most successful Automators share a crucial advantage: Arrowhead Brain State profiles. This optimal state allows them to:

- Handle complex technical challenges while maintaining focus
- See automation opportunities others miss
- Build more effective solutions faster than competitors

3. THE HUMAN-AI COACHES: THE CRITICAL LINK

Human-AI Coaches are pioneering a crucial new role in professional development. They help people maintain peak cognitive performance in a world where AI handles more routine mental tasks. Drawing on their understanding of Brain States and human performance, these coaches guide others to work at their best, especially during periods of intense cognitive demands. Just as athletic coaches help athletes optimize their physical performance, think of Human-AI Coaches as performance coaches for the mind in the AI era.

This is perhaps the most crucial role—the one Sarah found herself naturally growing into. Human-AI Coaches serve as essential guides in this transformation, with a twofold mission:

First, they must master their own Brain States, achieving and maintaining their own Arrowhead profile because:

- They model optimal performance for clients
- Clear thinking is essential for effective coaching and training
- They need sustained energy for deep coaching work and impactful delivery of training

Second, they guide others to peak performance, helping both Innovators and Automators develop and maintain Arrowhead profiles by:

- Teaching Brain State optimization techniques
- Supporting sustainable habit formation
- Ensuring premium cognitive performance when it matters most

THE HUMAN-AI EDGE

Think about what this means in practice.

When two Innovators compete to solve the same problem:

- The one with an Arrowhead profile has significantly more hours of premium cognitive performance daily
- They direct AI tools more effectively during High Charge states
- They consistently outperform those with fragmented Brain States

Similarly, when Automators compete to build automation solutions:

- Those with Arrowhead profiles see opportunities others miss
- They maintain focus through complex development challenges
- They create more effective solutions in less time

This is why Human-AI Coaches become essential. Their impact extends throughout organizations—from transforming individual performance to optimizing entire teams and guiding leaders through organizational change. They don't just help people use AI tools—they help optimize Brain States at every level, helping to create workplace cultures that make it easier for everyone to thrive in the AI Era.

Sarah found particular resonance with the Human-AI Coach role. "Looking at these three roles," she reflected, "I realized that helping others optimize their Brain States wasn't just something I enjoyed—it was becoming one of the most valuable skills in this new era."

YOUR PATH FORWARD

As Sarah discovered, understanding these emerging roles reveals extraordinary opportunities. Whether you're drawn to becoming an Innovator creating breakthroughs, an Automator building solutions, or aspiring to become a Human-AI Coach, your success depends on Brain State optimization.

In the next chapter, you'll discover how Sarah began helping others optimize their Brain States, providing a practical framework you can use whether you choose to become a coach yourself or simply want to help your team thrive in the AI era

27

TEACHING OTHERS TO THRIVE IN THE AI ERA

Sarah watched her colleague James staring at his screen, surrounded by the same AI tools that had once overwhelmed her. An accomplished engineer, James had the potential to be a brilliant Automator, but his fragmented Brain States were holding him back. "The frustration in his expression was all too familiar," she remembered. "That's when I knew—helping others optimize their Brain States wasn't just an opportunity, it was becoming essential."

This is where your journey expands beyond personal mastery. As organizations worldwide struggle to implement AI effectively, they're missing something crucial—experts who understand how to optimize human Brain States for this new way of working. This isn't about teaching people to use AI tools; it's about helping them build the habits that make human-AI collaboration natural and effective.

"The key to this method's success," Sarah observed, "was focusing on Brain States and habits rather than technology. Instead of another AI training session, I could show people how to match their natural energy patterns to different types of work, optimize their focus, and use AI tools strategically during different Brain States."

THREE LEVELS OF IMPACT THAT HUMAN-AI COACHES CAN MAKE:

1. Individual Optimization

- Helping others identify their optimal Brain States
- Guiding them to draft their first FAM Story and Will Power Story
- Supporting them as they craft their first Habit Building Plan

"I started with simple things," Sarah shared. "When I helped James create his first Will Power Story, we focused on identifying his natural High Charge times—those morning hours when his thinking was clearest. Just matching his important work to these peak times and using AI to handle routine tasks during energy dips transformed his productivity."

2. Team Integration

- Coordinating team Brain States for optimal collaboration
- Creating shared energy-aware meeting protocols
- Building supportive environments for High Charge work

"The power of team awareness became clear," Sarah explained. "Once everyone understood Brain States, they naturally started coordinating their collective energy patterns. They'd schedule creative meetings during shared High Charge times, used AI to handle routine tasks during energy dips, and planned coaching conversations when people had the right energy for deep thinking."

3. Cultural Transformation

- Embedding Brain States into organizational strategy and decision-making
- Creating company-wide policies that support Brain State energy optimization
- Building Brain State understanding into leadership development programs

"The real transformation happened to our workplace culture," Sarah explained. "Leaders began making Brain States part of our company DNA. They changed performance metrics to value energy management, invested in tools and training to support optimal Brain States, and recognized teams who consistently delivered high-impact work by matching tasks to their peak Brain States. More importantly, they created an environment where people felt safe to optimize their own performance and support others in doing the same."

COMMON CHALLENGES AND SOLUTIONS

As Sarah helped more people optimize their Brain States, she encountered several common challenges. Understanding these helps you support others more effectively:

1. **The Technology Focus Trap Challenge:** People fixating on AI tools rather than their Brain States.

Solution: Start with the Human-AI Readiness Brain State Assessment—once they see how their energy affects their work, AI's role becomes clearer.

2. **The Quick Fix Expectation Challenge:** Wanting immediate results without building habits.

Solution: Begin with tiny changes that show quick wins while building toward larger transformation.

3. **The All or Nothing Mindset Challenge:** Thinking they must master all AI tools immediately.

Solution: Focus on optimizing one Brain State at a time, gradually introducing AI support.

YOUR COACHING FRAMEWORK

1. Build Trust and Understanding

- Help map individual Brain State patterns
- Listen and show genuine care
- Understand current AI challenges

2. Guide Habit Development

- Start with personal Will Power Stories
- Connect daily habits to meaningful goals
- Create sustainable change plans

3. Establish Support Systems

- Regular check-in conversations
- Create accountability partnerships
- Build shared team practices

SARAH'S JOURNEY TO TEACHING

"At first, I just shared the Will Power Story tool," Sarah explained. "But I quickly realized the Success Cycle that transformed my own performance was exactly what others needed. I'd guide them through each step systematically:

First, we'd start with Measurement. I'd have them track their Brain States for a few days and complete the Human-AI Readiness Brain State Assessment, giving us a clear baseline of their current patterns and challenges.

Then came Planning with the Task Director. This was about more than just tasks—we'd start by creating their FAM Story, helping them see how optimizing their Brain States connected to their biggest goals and ambitions. Once they had that vision, we'd identify their ice sculptures and ice cubes, creating their first Will Power Story focused on optimizing their morning hours. Having their FAM Story made this planning more meaningful because they could see how each small improvement moved them toward their larger goals.

Next was Optimization with the Day Designer. Once they saw results from their morning routine, we'd gradually expand to designing their full day around their Brain States, matching tasks to energy levels and using AI tools strategically.

Finally, we'd focus on Automation with the Routine Engineer. We'd build triggers and systems using the Habit Building Plan framework that made their new patterns automatic rather than effortful. This was crucial for sustaining their transformation even during challenging periods."

"What amazed me was how this systematic approach worked whether I was coaching colleagues, entire teams, or senior leaders." Sarah explained. "The Success Cycle, anchored by the FAM Story, gave everyone a clear path from struggling with AI tools to thriving alongside them."

YOUR NEXT STEPS

Just as Sarah discovered, your journey to helping others is guided by the Success Cycle:

1. Start with Measurement

- Help your first person complete the Brain State Assessment
- Guide them in tracking their daily patterns
- Document their current AI tool challenges and opportunities

2. Move to Planning

Remember the Task Director's saying "The foundation determines the height."

- Guide them to drafting their FAM Story, and ice cube and ice sculpture lists
- Help them create their first Will Power Story, focusing on morning hours
- Show them how to match ice cube and ice sculpture tasks to Brain States

3. Progress to Optimization

Remember the Day Designer's saying "Planning transforms energy."

- Help them expand their Will Power Story to cover the full day
- Guide them in using AI tools strategically
- Help them design supportive environments for High Charge work

4: Build toward Automation

Remember the Routine Engineer's saying "Systems beat struggle."

- Develop triggers that make good habits automatic
- Help them create their first Habit Building Plan
- Help them build resilient routines that last

Remember, your role isn't to be a technical expert. You're a guide helping others optimize their most valuable asset—their Brain States—in an AI-augmented world. As you master this process with individuals, you can expand to teams and eventually whole organizations. As Sarah discovered: "When you help someone master their Brain States and build effective habits, you don't just improve their performance—you transform their life!"

28

UNDERSTANDING BRAIN STATES AT SCALE: CREATING BRAIN STATE INTELLIGENT CULTURES

A s we conclude our exploration of Brain States and AI integration, let's step back and examine a transformative opportunity that few organizations have yet recognized.

Throughout this book, we've focused on optimizing your individual cognitive performance. In doing so we've revealed something profound about happiness in the AI era. It's not just about using technology to get more done—it's about using it strategically to create the right mix of Recharge, routine work, and high-impact, high-value work that allows you to do your job and live your life in a way that leads to lasting satisfaction.

Now let's understand how these same principles can revolutionize entire organizations by unleashing healthy, happy, and high-performing workforces.

As artificial intelligence transforms business, a powerful opportunity is emerging: organizations can dramatically improve performance by aligning work patterns with how human brains naturally function. This quickly creates measurable improvements by helping teams to complete key projects over 200% faster. This is only possible when organizations optimize how their people perform alongside powerful AI tools.

This optimization comes through creating what we call '**Brain State Intelligent Cultures**'—our Six Sigma for human performance in the AI era. But to successfully create these winning cultures we need to first consider the barriers.

THE CURRENT STATE OF PLAY

AI is transforming business at an unprecedented pace. According to the World Economic Forum's recent *Future of Jobs Report*, 86% of companies expect AI to revolutionize their operations. Yet, this transformation brings serious challenges. Successful AI adoption isn't just about deploying new technology—it requires a fundamental shift in how humans and AI collaborate.

Many organizations underestimate the cognitive toll this shift takes on their workforce. The cognitive demands of rapid technological change and our increasingly volatile, uncertain, complex and ambiguous world are pushing employees to their cognitive limits, leading to a cascade of business risks:

- **Employee engagement nosedives** under relentless cognitive strain.
- **Mental fatigue surges** as workers struggle to keep up with constant technological change.
- **Learning capacity collapses** under information overload, stalling critical projects.
- **Team effectiveness deteriorates** as digital overload fragments communication and collaboration.

- **Innovation grinds to a halt** when employees can't maintain deep, focused thinking.
- **Workplace wellbeing suffers**, driving higher staff turnover and making it harder to retain top talent.

If businesses fail to address these cognitive challenges, the consequences will be severe: declining productivity, stalled innovation, and an exodus of skilled employees. The future of work isn't just about adopting AI—it's about ensuring humans can thrive alongside it.

These challenges become particularly acute during major organizational transformations. As an example of the difficulties businesses face during major transitions, let's consider mergers and acquisitions (M&A): companies spend more than $2 trillion annually on M&A deals, yet 70-90% fail to meet expectations. While traditional analysis blames factors like poor strategic fit or incorrect valuations, a deeper truth emerges: combining cultures, systems, and AI technologies creates overwhelming cognitive demands that most organizations aren't equipped to handle. Without optimizing Brain States, even the most strategically sound transformations can fail as people struggle to maintain the focused thinking needed to implement complex change.

These observations aren't just theoretical—they're built on my twenty-five years of developing a fundamentally different approach to helping individuals, teams, and leaders optimize their cognitive performance during challenging transitions. Through working with over 20,000 people and completing my PhD in this area, I've seen these challenges firsthand. But I've also seen something else: when organizations understand how to optimize Brain States, extraordinary transformations become possible.

THE POWER OF FIRST PRINCIPLES THINKING

To appreciate what's possible, consider how sports science transformed physical athletic performance. Twenty-five years ago, I worked on the frontlines of this revolution, watching as teams abandoned traditional training approaches in favour of methods based on how the human body actually functions. The transformation wasn't about working harder—it was about aligning training with the body's fundamental mechanics.

Today, we face a similar opportunity with cognitive performance through Brain State optimization. As I've shown throughout this book, over the past 25 years, we've developed a deep proprietary understanding of how to translate cutting-edge insights from neuroscience and behavioral science into practical organizational change.

Just as sports scientists created systems that teams could implement in their daily training, we've developed methodologies that help businesses seamlessly integrate brain science into their daily practices. This systematic approach allows organizations to create cultures where optimal cognitive performance becomes natural rather than forced. And just as sports science created a new standard for athletic excellence, this integration of human cognitive optimization with technological capability **creates the need for something unprecedented in organizational performance: Brain State Intelligent Cultures.** The result of this new approach isn't just better performance—it's the kind of environment where both people and technology can work together at their best.

THE HOLY GRAIL: BRAIN STATE INTELLIGENT CULTURES

I believe that teams and organizations that create these cultures will thrive in the AI Era and therefore creating one should be every business's number one goal. In these environments technology enhances rather than overwhelms human capabilities, and sustainable high-performance emerges from aligning work with how brains actually function.

A Brain State Intelligent Culture transforms performance across every level of you organization:

Young Professionals:

- **Become productive revenue drivers faster** by mastering complex skills and AI tools in months instead of years.
- **Build long-term sustainable high performance** by managing stress effectively, increasing their impact.
- **Stay engaged and grow within the company,** improving retention and maximizing long-term potential.

Middle Managers:

- **Drive faster AI adoption and ROI** by confidently leading change and turning resistance into measurable productivity gains.
- **Deliver on strategic initiatives while maintaining team performance,** balancing competing demands without burnout.
- **Create high-performing teams that consistently hit targets** by optimizing both personal and collective productivity.

Senior Leaders:

- **Make sharper strategic decisions for longer** using science-backed strategies from elite performance—maintaining peak cognitive function throughout their careers.
- **Drive successful AI transformation** by mastering the human factors that accelerate adoption and maximize ROI.

- **Create lasting cultural change** that turns resistance into enthusiasm, fostering sustained high performance across the organization.

Teams:

- **Deliver complex projects over 200% faster** by optimizing collective brain function for breakthrough performance.
- **Maintain peak productivity during AI transformation** by aligning work patterns with natural energy cycles—preventing costly burnout.
- **Drive faster innovation and problem-solving** by enabling seamless collaboration across generations and skill levels.

These individual and team improvements combine to create powerful organizational outcomes: reduced burnout, lower staff turnover, enhanced innovation, better talent retention, and improved customer solutions. Most importantly, they create environments where people genuinely want to stay and grow because they can consistently perform at their best without sacrificing wellbeing—this creates a powerful competitive advantage. But achieving this transformation isn't a matter of chance—it requires a systematic understanding of how lasting change happens in organizations.

THE NINE ESSENTIAL ELEMENTS

Just as Six Sigma transformed manufacturing and quality management in the industrial era, Brain State Intelligence will revolutionize human performance in the AI era. While Six Sigma optimized production processes, our nine interconnected factors optimize something even more fundamental—how human brains function alongside AI technology.

Creating this 'Brain State' transformation requires understanding these nine factors that behavioral science shows drive sustainable change. These factors work together like an orchestra—each instrument matters, but the real magic happens when they play in harmony.

Here are the nine factors from our proprietary system (I first introduced these in chapter 23):

1. **Brain State Optimization:** Creating environments where people can maintain optimal cognitive states
2. **Habit Mechanic Mindset:** Cultivating belief in continuous improvement
3. **Tiny Change Factor:** Making transformation manageable
4. **Personal Motivation:** Connecting small changes to bigger personal and professional goals
5. **Personal Knowledge and Skills:** Building individual capabilities
6. **Community Knowledge:** Developing shared practices
7. **Social Influence:** Leveraging natural behavior spread
8. **Rewards and Penalties:** Aligning incentive systems with desired behaviors
9. **External Triggers:** Designing supportive environments that remind people how to be their best

BUILDING SYSTEMATIC CHANGE

Creating a Brain State Intelligent Culture requires careful integration of all nine factors into daily organizational practices. This isn't about implementing isolated initiatives—it's about building reinforcing cycles where each improvement strengthens the others. Organizations that master this systematic approach will achieve breakthrough results, just as Six Sigma became the gold standard for manufacturing excellence.

LOOKING FORWARD

The AI revolution presents every organization with a choice: optimize how your people work alongside these powerful tools, or risk falling behind those who do. Leading organizations are already building Brain State Intelligent Cultures, setting new standards for what's possible when human potential and technological capability work in harmony.

The question isn't whether your organization will need to make this transition. The question is: Will you be among the pioneers who lead this change and create an insurmountable lead, or will you get left behind?

29

FREE RESOURCES, FAST-TRACK TRAINING, AND CERTIFICATIONS

Whether you're seeking to optimize your own performance, transform your team, pioneer Brain State intelligence at scale, or become a Human-AI Coach helping others thrive, our proven 30-day programs help you immediately implement everything you've learned in this book.

We offer three core ways to begin your journey:

1. SELF-PACED RESOURCES

The Habit Mechanic Podcast

Get weekly insights and accountability for implementing the Success Cycle. Each episode provides practical tools and tips for creating real results. Listen at <u>tougherminds.co.uk/podcast</u> or search for 'Habit Mechanic' on any mainstream podcast app.

Habit Mechanic University App

Join the community, play the Brain State Games, access over 30 habit building tools, and track your progress—all designed to help you achieve your big goals faster. Download at tougherminds.co.uk.

2. EXPERT COACHING AND TEAM TRAINING

Keynote Speaking

Inspire your audience with powerful insights on Brain State optimization and AI integration. Our keynotes bring the Success Cycle to life for conferences, company events, and leadership gatherings.

Individual Coaching

Work directly with a certified Habit Mechanic AI-Edge coach in focused 30-day cycles. See powerful results in your first month as you learn to optimize your Brain States and work strategically with AI tools. Each cycle builds on the last, helping you achieve your biggest goals faster.

Team Training and Leadership Development

We help teams and businesses create 'Brain State Intelligent Cultures' (our Six Sigma for human performance in the AI era) that unlock what's possible when human potential and AI work in harmony. Our clients consistently complete key projects over 200% faster by optimizing how their people perform alongside powerful AI tools.

We offer three levels of training and certifications: for C-Suite and senior leaders; team leaders; and team members.

Your teams will quickly see measurable improvements.

All programs are customized to your organization's needs through coaching, workshops, webinars, or comprehensive certification programs. The results? Reduced burnout, enhanced innovation, better talent retention, and improved solutions for your customers. Most importantly, we create environments where people want to stay and grow because they can consistently perform at their best without sacrificing wellbeing—giving you a powerful competitive advantage.

3. BECOME A CERTIFIED PROFESSIONAL

Habit Mechanic AI-Edge Coach

Help others achieve their goals faster through our proven 30-day coaching system.

Habit Mechanic AI-Edge Trainer

Join our select network of certified trainers implementing these methods in organizations worldwide.

READY TO BEGIN?

We accept a limited number of clients each month to ensure premium support.

For information about any of these programs, contact us at:

contact@tougherminds.co.uk

Or via our website:

tougherminds.co.uk

CONCLUSION

READY TO LEAD THE AI REVOLUTION?

As artificial intelligence transforms how we work, a crucial truth is emerging: the key to thriving in the AI era isn't mastering every new AI tool—it's mastering your Brain States. When you optimize your natural cognitive rhythms, and build effective habits, your optimized cognitive performance turns AI tools into powerful allies rather than overwhelming burdens.

Through the Success Cycle, you've learned to measure your Brain State patterns, match tasks to your natural energy patterns, use AI strategically during different Brain States, optimize the rhythm of your day, and make excellence automatic. These tools don't just help you adapt to the AI era— they position you to shape its future.

Whether you began with a Cross to Bear, Jagged Jewel, or Arrowhead profile, you now have the tools to transform your cognitive performance and help others do the same.

The AI Revolution creates an unprecedented opportunity to transform Brain State management and achieve sustainable high performance for individuals, teams, and organizations.Your journey as a master of Brain States begins now. The world needs your optimized mind and unique value.

The AI Revolution is here, and you're ready to lead it!

AND FINALLY...

A Request to Help Others

If this book has helped you, please share it with someone else. We need all the help we can get in helping humans to thrive in the AI Revolution. Your leadership starts with teaching others what you've learned.

Spread the word.

Thank you!

APPENDICES

The following appendices represent a deliberate bridge between practical implementation and deeper understanding. They are carefully selected chapters from my best-selling book 'The Habit Mechanic'—our comprehensive guide to understanding and optimizing how your brain works, how to be your best, and how to lead others to be their best.

While 'Train Your Brain for the AI Revolution' focuses on immediate application, we've chosen these specific chapters from The Habit Mechanic because they provide crucial scientific foundations that will deepen your success with Brain State optimization. Each appendix builds upon the next, creating a complete picture of how your brain processes information, manages emotions, and builds lasting habits.

This progressive structure is intentional:

- Appendix A introduces the fundamental neuroscience of your brain
- Appendix B explores how activation levels connect to Brain States
- Appendix C illuminates the mechanics of habit formation
- Appendix D reveals how the Nine Action Factors framework brings everything together

Even if you've read The Habit Mechanic, seeing these concepts through the lens of AI-era challenges creates powerful new insights. Just as your brain builds stronger neural connections through repeated exposure in different contexts, revisiting these foundational principles while focusing on AI optimization helps cement your understanding and reveals new applications.

Understanding these deeper principles will enhance your appreciation of the Brain State optimization techniques presented in the main book, while showing how they connect to broader principles of human performance and wellbeing. More importantly, this scientific foundation will help you adapt these principles as AI technology continues to evolve.

Note: When specific chapter numbers appear in parentheses within these appendices (e.g., "Chapter 10"), they reference chapters from 'The Habit Mechanic' book, not this current book.

APPENDIX A

THE FUNDAMENTAL NEUROSCIENCE OF YOUR BRAIN

While the main text focuses on practical Brain State optimization for the AI era, this appendix explores the fundamental neuroscience of how your brain processes information and regulates emotions. Drawing from The Habit Mechanic, this detailed exploration introduces foundational concepts like the 'Lighthouse Brain' model with HUE (Horribly Unhelpful Emotions), Will Power, and the distinction between the APE (Alive, Perceived, Energy) Brain and HAC (Helpful Attention Control) Brain.

Understanding these basics of brain function and emotional regulation provides the scientific foundation for why optimizing your Brain States is so crucial. Just as a mechanic needs to understand how an engine works before optimizing its performance, professionals in the AI era need to understand their brain's natural tendencies and emotional regulation systems to effectively manage their mental energy and build lasting habits.

9

HOW YOUR
BRAIN WORKS

HOW CAN I ACTUALLY START DOING BETTER?
TRY ME POWER CONDITIONING

Each of us can choose to take responsibility for our wellbeing and performance, and purposefully work toward being at our best.

If we think in terms of a scale, at one end we could *refuse* to try to be at our best. This means that you are passive and let the VUCA world control you and what you learn to become good at. This can result in people getting really good at lots of unhelpful things. I call this end of the scale "VUCA World Conditioning." If you want to lose the Learning War, *refusing* to try to be at your best will guarantee it!

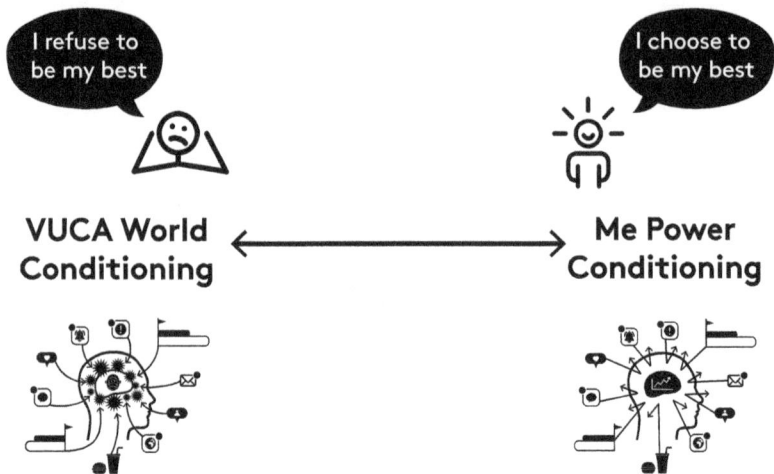

Figure 9.1: The Best Doing continuum.

At the opposite end of the scale, we could purposefully *choose* to work toward being at our best. It turns out that choosing to be at your best gives you a much better chance not only of fulfilling your potential but also of being happy.

I call deliberately choosing to do this "Me Power Conditioning." Learning how to do this is at the heart of becoming a Habit Mechanic.

To help you do more Me Power Conditioning, I want to help you understand more about how you think. We pay attention to things by thinking about them, and this leads to learning. In other words, attention drives learning.

THINKING ABOUT YOUR THINKING

First, let's take a few moments to consider how we think.

The aim of this exercise is to highlight that we are always thinking. Recognizing that fact is an important part of the Me Power Conditioning process. Our brain is always on: it's designed to keep paying attention.

However, our attention span is naturally short—and it's becoming shorter because of how we use it in the modern world. We can think of our brains as "frog brains" that jump from one thing to another.

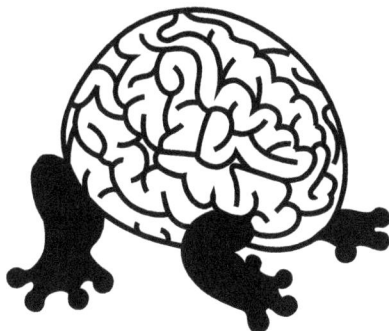

Figure 9.2: The attention economy is shortening our attention span and making it more difficult to focus.

Our brains are designed to pay attention to things that bring us short-term gratification (pleasure). This can stop us achieving long-term objectives that would bring truly great satisfaction and fulfillment (personal growth).

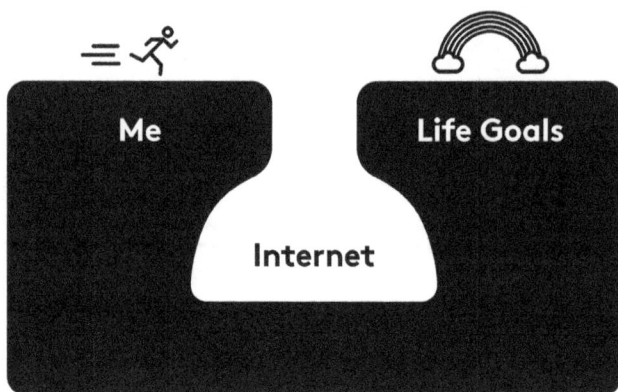

Figure 9.3: Even with the best intentions to get things done, it is easier than ever to get sidetracked.

Remember, the more we think and do unhelpful things, the better we become at them.

These unhelpful behaviors (thoughts and actions) also make us less efficient and effective. For example, it feels easier than ever to spend 10 minutes doing a task that we could do in five minutes because we become easily distracted by our smartphones or emails. It also feels easier than ever to waste time beating ourselves up.

Figure 9.4: It is easy to waste a lot of time each day doing and thinking unhelpful things.

By the end of the day, we find we've lost 30 minutes. And by the end of the week, we are three hours down. We will never get this time back. We will probably have to stay at work later, spend less time with our loved ones, and beat ourselves up even more as a result. We find ourselves trapped in a negative cycle. But it doesn't have to be this way. We can all strike a better balance between work and home life by learning how to do more Me Power Conditioning, so we build more helpful habits.

HOW DO YOU USE YOUR DAY?

All of us have just 24 hours in any single day. We can be doing (and thinking) either things that are helping us achieve our health, happiness, and performance goals, or things that are unhelpful and stopping us from achieving them. Think of it like a barcode (see Figure 9.5): The white lines represent helpful thoughts and actions (e.g., sleeping properly, doing focused work, speaking to yourself in a positive way, practicing your stress management skills). The black lines represent when you are doing and thinking things that are unhelpful for your health, happiness, and performance (e.g., beating yourself up, eating the wrong foods, procrastinating, staying up too late). To be at our best more often, we need to get better at recognizing our unhelpful behaviors and removing one unhelpful black line at a time.

Figure 9.5: I will show you how to identify your black lines and eradicate them one at a time.

"HELPFUL VERSUS UNHELPFUL"— NOT "POSITIVE VERSUS NEGATIVE"

It is important to say that **helpful thinking** is NOT necessarily the same as **positive thinking**, and **unhelpful thinking** is NOT necessarily the same as **negative thinking**. For example, receiving negative feedback about something you are trying to improve can be really helpful (e.g., if delivered in the right way, it will help you improve). Eating a donut every morning for breakfast (which if you like them will be a VERY positive experience) can be really unhelpful (e.g., it might make it more difficult to achieve your weight loss or healthy eating goals).

But why is it so easy to think and do unhelpful things? To understand this, we need to consider how our brains work.

I am going to show you how your brain works using three different but interconnected models. They range from simple to complex.

1. Simple—Lighthouse Brain
2. Intermediate—APE Brain vs. HAC Brain
3. Complex—Emotional Regulation

> *I created the insights I am about to share to make it as easy as possible to understand how we can all begin to spend more time doing and thinking more helpful things, by building more helpful habits.*

10

THE LIGHTHOUSE
BRAIN

We might know what we want to do or achieve, but accomplishing it is a different story. To help you understand why, I want to tell you a story about how your brain works. The concepts in this will be the basis for everything else that follows in this book. They will provide a solid foundation so you can understand exactly how you, or you and your team, can fulfill your potential. I've created this story to make complex psychology, neuroscience, and behavioral science easy to understand. I will provide more details about the science later.

Figure 10.1: The Lighthouse Brain.

First, imagine you have a lighthouse in your brain. Two characters live there. The first is HUE. This stands for Horribly Unhelpful Emotions. The second is Willomenia Power, or Will Power for short. Most importantly, Will Power is HUE's guide and mentor.

HUE

HUE works in the lighthouse's control room. Its first instinct is to search for threats. Imagine HUE using a beam of light emitted from the lighthouse to mindlessly scan your thoughts, your feelings, and the environment around you. It scans for past mistakes or regrets. It projects worst-case scenarios about what might happen in the future. And it searches for any immediate problems.

HUE's second instinct is to find easy, new, and exciting things that make it feel good. HUE loves doing things and having experiences that give it short-term gratification.

Figure 10.2: Meet your Horribly Unhelpful Emotions (HUE).

WILL POWER

There is a training room in the lighthouse. Will Power likes to learn about how to help you fulfill your potential and spends most of its time in there, studying and learning. When HUE notices a problem, or a short-term gratification opportunity, it sometimes calls Will Power for help. When everything in your brain is working properly, Will Power guides HUE to solve the problem or manage unhelpful impulses.

This makes it easier for HUE to deal with similar problems if they occur again.

Figure 10.3: Meet Willomenia Power, or Will Power, HUE's guide and mentor.

The Will Power Mentoring process looks something like this:

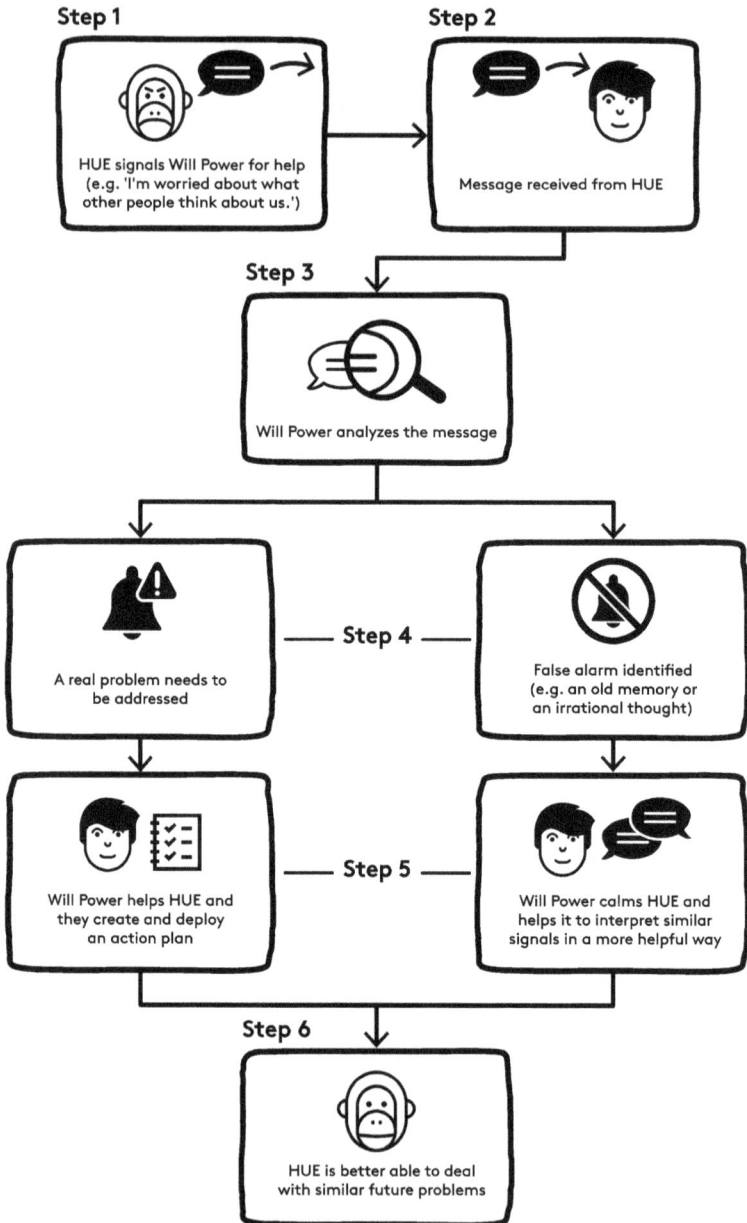

Step 1
HUE signals Will Power for help (e.g. 'I'm worried about what other people think about us.')

Step 2
Message received from HUE

Step 3
Will Power analyzes the message

Step 4
A real problem needs to be addressed

False alarm identified (e.g. an old memory or an irrational thought)

Step 5
Will Power helps HUE and they create and deploy an action plan

Will Power calms HUE and helps it to interpret similar signals in a more helpful way

Step 6
HUE is better able to deal with similar future problems

Figure 10.4: A simple overview of how Will Power and HUE can work together successfully.

When Will Power can do its job properly, your HUE will be calmer, and it should be easier for you to:

- build good diet, exercise, and sleep habits;
- successfully manage stress;
- spend less time thinking unhelpful thoughts;
- build and maintain robust levels of confidence;
- be focused, productive, creative, and good at solving problems;
- perform well under pressure;
- be a better leader; and
- be a better team member.

"Calmer HUE, better you."

But, as I have already shown, the modern world presents many new challenges that can overwhelm us.

- We can find it hard to switch off, which can negatively affect sleep, rest, and recovery.
- Social media leads us to compare our lives to others', and we can beat ourselves up too much.
- We are tempted to eat bad food, buy things we don't need, and spend money we don't have.
- We become distracted, so a 10-minute job takes 20 minutes. Over a week, this accumulates into several wasted hours.

These types of challenges result in an unhelpful imbalance between HUE and Will Power. HUE can become overactivated, and Will Power can quickly get overwhelmed and exhausted. This makes it very difficult to be healthy, happy, and at your best.

If you want to win the Learning War, be your best, and help others do the same, your first job is to get HUE and Will Power working together efficiently and effectively, creating more balance between these two powerful assets.

To help you do this, let's dig deeper into the inner workings of your brain.

Test?

If it is helpful, write down what HUE stands for to test your memory!

11

WHAT ACTUALLY HAPPENS INSIDE MY BRAIN?

O bviously, there isn't really a lighthouse in your brain! I created this story to make some very complex processes easy to understand. Let me explain in more detail what is going on.

HUE

HUE operates the limbic regions of the brain. I call these areas the APE (**A**live, **P**erceived, and **E**nergy) Brain. This was partly inspired by neuro-scientist Paul MacLean's seminal "triune brain" metaphor, and also the fact that Homo sapiens (humans) are Great Apes. The APE Brain makes us prioritize survival.

Note: I sometimes use the terms "APE Brain" and "HUE" interchangeably.

WILL POWER

Will Power operates the prefrontal cortex, or the HAC (**H**elpful **A**ttention **C**ontrol) Brain (pronounced *hack* brain). We can use the HAC Brain to manage the APE Brain and build better habits.

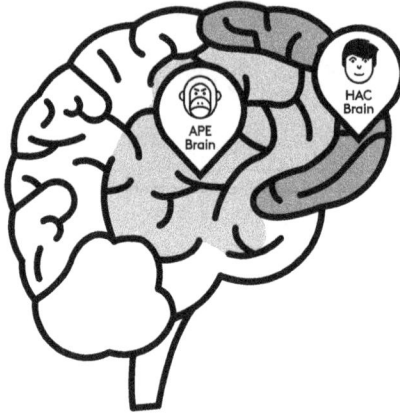

Figure 11.1: A cartoon drawing of the human brain to show the broad regions where the APE and HAC Brains are located in my model.

YOUR APE BRAIN PRIORITIZES SAVING ENERGY, MAKING CHANGE DIFFICULT

To understand more about the APE Brain, please read aloud the following passage.

To make sense of words it deosn't mttaer in what order the ltteers in a wrod are, the olny ipmoratnt tihng is taht the frist and lsat ltteer are in the rghit pclae.

Even though the letters are mixed up, you can still understand the meaning. This is because most of our thoughts and actions (behaviors) are mindless. We mainly guess and predict. In fact, science shows that at least 98 percent of our behavior is unconscious or semi-unconscious, meaning it is habit.

You have the equivalent of over one trillion microscopic biological moving parts in your brain that mindlessly drive most of what you do and think.

So you did not need to read the passage consciously, taking the time to process each individual letter in each word. Your brain reads each word as a picture, meaning that even if some of the letters are not in the correct place, the picture still makes sense.

Because habits make thinking and doing things more energy efficient, we have evolved to run on them. This means we do not think about most of the things we do.

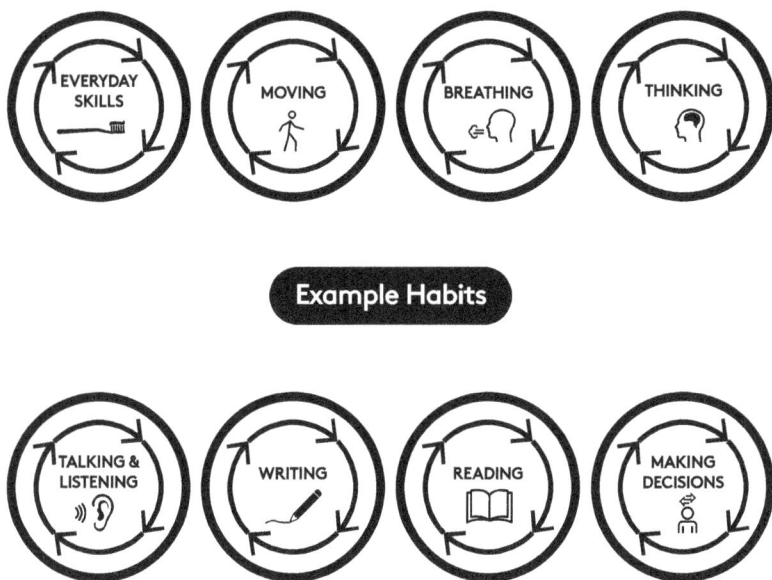

Figure 11.2: Examples of everyday things you do that are mainly habit.

Our habits dominate what we do and how we think. Our experience of the world is what we are in the habit of paying attention to. For example, if we only pay attention to our failures in life and the setbacks we've experienced, that becomes our reality. Equally, if we only pay attention to how fantastic we think we are, and how nothing is ever our fault, that becomes our reality.

Our family, friends, colleagues, teams, and organizations all run on habits. The most dominant habits are those they practice most, because of the process I explained earlier known as neuroplasticity.

Some of our habits are helpful for us being at our best, and some are unhelpful.

We Are Not Designed to Be Healthy, Happy, and at Our Best

Homo sapiens have been around for about 300,000 years. Our primal instincts, driven by our APE Brain, mean we are not designed to be happy and at our best in the context of our 21st century lives.

Alive

Instead, we are designed to survive. To stay Alive, we prioritize all the things that are essential for doing that. Although for most people things like food, shelter, and warmth are a given in the modern world, notice how quickly the supermarket shelves emptied during the COVID-19 pandemic.

We are also instinctively concerned about our physical safety. Notice your reaction to a loud bang or a stranger getting too close to you, or your heightened sensitivity to shadows in the dark after watching a horror movie.

Perceived

Closely connected to staying alive is our concern about how we are **Perceived** by other people who are important in our lives—think social status, peer pressure, and how social media is used. Communication, cooperation, and alliances with other humans support our survival. Humans are not the biggest or strongest animal on the planet, but they are the best at working intelligently in teams. Teamwork has been the foundation of human survival and success (i.e., historically, if you got kicked out of the team or the tribe, your survival chances were significantly reduced, as were your chances of passing on your genes). Our success in life can be closely connected to how we are viewed by people who are important in our lives. So, we often worry too much about what others think.

Energy

Finally, as food—our main source of energy—has not always been readily available (i.e., we used to be hunters and gatherers, and not supermarket shoppers), we make every effort to conserve **Energy**. This is why we sometimes prefer to sit and watch TV instead of exercising, and we avoid work that is mentally challenging. Thinking hard burns a lot of energy! For example, it will take less mental energy to perform a well-practiced task than it will to learn a new skill or perform a difficult task.

We can even see this in our food preferences. Your brain knows that it is more energy efficient to eat a donut than an apple. It takes just as much energy to eat both, but there are more calories in the donut.

Survival Habits

The collective APE result is what I call "survival habits." Here are some examples:

- Worrying too much
- Being unfairly self-critical or beating yourself up
- Giving in to temptation
- Easily getting distracted
- Procrastinating
- Giving up easily
- Jumping to conclusions
- Easily becoming stressed

These habits operate like any other: the more you practice, the better you get. For example, if you want to get better at worrying, all you have to do is practice worrying a lot and you will become a world champion worrier. This is because the more you practice it, the more you grow and strengthen the neurons in your brain that are connected to worrying.

In the Learning War, these types of habits are becoming increasingly problematic because of the challenges we face in the VUCA world. These unhelpful habits mean we can beat ourselves up too much or procrastinate on things that we really do need to get done.

In fact, these habits are often the biggest waste of personal resources in any 24-hour period.

And if they are the biggest waste of resources for an individual, they are also the biggest waste of resources for a team, business, or family unit.

Think back to the black and white barcode (Chapter 9, Figure 9.5). The white lines represent helpful habits and the black lines represent unhelpful habits (the barriers to your happiness and success).

Habits underpin everything we do:

- How we think and feel
- What we eat
- How much we exercise
- How well we sleep
- How we manage stress
- Our confidence levels
- How productive we are
- Our creativity and problem-solving abilities
- Our performance under pressure
- Our performance as a leader
- Our performance as a team member
- Our performance as a parent

If we want to be at our best more often, individually and collectively, we need to learn how to build more new helpful habits.

The first step to building new habits is called "intelligent Self-Watching." The Daily TEA Plan (Chapter 1) and the Daily 3:1 Reflection (Chapter 5) both require you to do intelligent Self-Watching. Let's do some more now.

Test?

If it is helpful, write down what APE and HAC stand for to test your memory!

12

HOW TO START ME POWER CONDITIONING

To start identifying some of your unhelpful habits, I want you to do some intelligent Self-Watching. This simply means thinking about yourself in a focused and systematic way, so that you can precisely identify your unhelpful behavior. This can be difficult to do because you are designed to run on habits.

Figure 12.1: Self-Watching is like switching on a CCTV camera that monitors your thoughts and actions.

To help you do this, I have created a short "APE Brain Test."

There are no right or wrong answers. This is just about what you think about yourself right now. The more you practice Self-Watching exercises like the APE Brain Test, the better you will become at understanding yourself. I complete this type of test about once a month to help me stay on top of my APE Brain. The more I practice intelligent Self-Watching, the better I get.

You could complete the test either from your own point of view, or on behalf of a person you want to help. Score each statement from 1 to 10, where 1 equals never and 10 equals always.

Note: It doesn't matter what your scores are. The important thing is that you are thinking about yourself and identifying your strengths and areas for improvement. Don't overthink your scores; just go with your gut instinct. The more you practice intelligent Self-Watching, the better you will get at it.

1. I reflect on my diet, exercise, and sleep, and plan to make daily improvements in these areas. *Score:* _____
2. At the end of the day, I always reflect and highlight what went well, and what I can improve tomorrow. *Score:* _____
3. At the end of every week, I reflect on what went well, and plan how I can improve next week. *Score:* _____
4. From time to time, I think about my future. I set long-, medium-, and short-term goals to focus my efforts and achieve major objectives. *Score:* _____
5. I regularly update my yearly and monthly calendar to add important work and life activities. *Score:* _____
6. I recognize when I'm stressed and successfully plan to reduce my stress. *Score:* _____
7. I monitor my confidence levels and successfully build up confidence in areas where it is low. *Score:* _____

8. I recognize when my emotions are unhelpful and can successfully keep them under control. *Score:* _____
9. I successfully plan to improve my productivity levels. *Score:* _____
10. I successfully plan to spend less time dwelling on unhelpful thoughts. *Score:* _____
11. I successfully plan to improve my performance as a leader. *Score:* _____

What next?

1. Circle the area you think it will be most helpful to make a small adjustment to today to help you be your best.
2. Write down one small thing you will do differently to improve this area.

> *(Tip: Writing "Be less stressed" is too vague to be helpful. Instead, be more specific—e.g., "Write a 3:1 Daily Reflection at the end of the working day.")*

_____

_____

_____

3. Explain why (e.g., "It will make it easier to de-stress, switch off, sleep well, and be at my best tomorrow").

_____

_____

_____

Don't worry if you are not sure how to improve the area you have selected, because I am going to cover all of the core APE Brain Test themes throughout the remainder of the book.

Although this book has been written to be read sequentially, you can jump ahead to get some improvement ideas—if you promise to come back to this point in the book and continue reading 😄. I have listed where you can learn more about each core APE Brain Test area below:

- I want to improve my sleep and/or diet and/or exercise. (Chapter 19)
- I want to improve my long-, medium-, and short-term goal setting. (Chapter 16)
- I want to get better at managing stress and thinking more helpfully. (Chapter 22)
- I want to improve my confidence. (Chapter 23)
- I want to get better at performing under pressure. (Chapter 24)
- I want to improve my focus and productivity. (Chapter 25)
- I want to improve my leadership. (Step 4—Chief Habit Mechanic skills)

If you do jump ahead, remember that the key to Habit Mechanic success is learning how to build sustainable new habits. Knowing what you need to do is very different from doing it. For the remainder of this section of the book (Step 2) and the beginning of the next (Step 3), I am going to really get under the hood (or bonnet) of what it takes to develop more new sustainable helpful habits.

But first, I want to finish this chapter by introducing a concept called the "Me Power Wish List."

By taking the APE Brain Test, you will have identified the most significant challenge(s) or problem(s) your APE Brain poses in your life right now. (If you complete it again next month, the scores might be different because your life circumstances and habits might be a little bit different.)

You may now want to begin creating your Me Power Wish List. This is a list of all the small new helpful habits you would like to build and changes you would like to make based on your APE Brain Test results.

YOUR ME POWER WISH LIST

Create your list where it is most helpful for you, for example, a notebook, Word file, phone note.

Please remember it's only realistically possible to **make one tiny change/ build one tiny new habit at a time**. This is a wish list for a reason: nobody has the resources to make all the changes they want at once.

I have a list of daily, weekly, and monthly habits I developed over many years that started on my Me Power Wish List and are now cables in my brain. Remember: knowing (knowledge), to doing (skill), to habit.

EXAMPLE ME POWER WISH LIST

Daily

- 6.30 a.m. run (if this sounds too difficult, you could go for a five-minute walk instead)
- Core—40 push-ups and 40 sit-ups (if this sounds too difficult, you could start with one push-up)
- Stretch
- Post my Daily TEA Plan in my Habit Mechanic app
- Will Power Boosters (e.g., one fewer check of my phone, apps off my phone, phone off, no TV news during the week, no emails at night) (learn more in Chapter 25)
- Drink two liters of water per day
- Aim for approximately eight miles of running/walking per day
- End-of-day positive reflection/Expressive Writing (learn more in Chapter 22)
- Complete my "Me Power Weekly Wall Chart" goals for the day (learn more in Chapter 18)

Weekly

- Structured weekly reflection (learn more in Chapter 36)
- Plan week ahead using Brain States method (learn more in Chapter 25)
- Create my Me Power Weekly Wall Chart (learn more in Chapter 18)

Monthly

- Habit review (learn more in Chapter 17)
- "Future Ambitious Meaningful Story" review (learn more in Chapter 16)
- "Team Power Leadership" review (learn more in Step 4)

> *Next, let's think about what happened in your brain as you were completing the APE Brain Test.*

13

USING WILL POWER
TO SELF-WATCH, HAC,
AND DEVELOP RESILIENCE

I n my model, the prefrontal cortex is the HAC (Helpful Attention Control) Brain. We can use it to manage the APE (Alive Perceived Energy) Brain. We imagine the HAC Brain is operated by Will Power.

Will Power is our first line of defense against the APE Brain because it allows us to resist temptations (e.g., eating too much junk food) and distractions (e.g., checking our social media).

WHAT IS RESILIENCE?

Using your Will Power to HAC (pronounced "hack") your brain is a two-step process:

Step 1. Regular Self-Watching to help you recognize when you are doing and thinking things that are unhelpful and that make it more difficult for you to be at your best (e.g., recognizing that you are beating yourself up too much).

Step 2. Refocusing your attention* onto things that are more helpful and make it easier for you to be at your best (e.g., focusing on thoughts that make you feel more positive about yourself).

I find the most powerful way to refocus my attention is to write down my thoughts, that is, create a written reflection or plan (I will say more about this in Chapter 22).

The outcome of this two-step process is **resilience**. So being resilient is an outcome you can achieve in this way. And this is exactly what you did when you completed the APE Brain Test in the last chapter. You highlighted your unhelpful behavior (i.e., by answering the test questions), and then you focused your attention onto doing something that was more helpful for you (e.g., completing a Daily 3:1 Reflection at the end of each day to help you de-stress).

Like anything else, resilience is something we can all learn to improve. We just need to practice it properly.

Resilience makes it easier to

- build better habits;
- be healthier;
- be happier;
- persist;
- manage stress effectively;
- increase your confidence;
- focus your attention;
- be more efficient and effective;
- be a better problem solver;
- be more creative;
- perform better under pressure; and
- be an outstanding leader.

When you HAC your brain to activate your resilience, you are actually managing your emotions. The centrality of emotions during this process is evident when we look at the different terms different scientists use to describe what I call HACing (pronounced "hacking").

- Social scientists call this emotional self-control.
- Neuroscientists call this emotional regulation.

Whichever term you use to describe the process, the outcome is the same: it helps people manage their emotions so they can be more resilient.

RESILIENCE IS LIKE YOUR
SWISS ARMY KNIFE FOR LIFE SUCCESS

Many preeminent scientists have studied this process since the 1960s and large sets of compelling research data have been collected about its importance.

Professor Roy Baumeister is one of the world's most respected and prolific social psychologists. His work has been cited by other academics over 200,000 times, he has over 650 publications, and he has written 40 books.

He lists the outcomes you are far more likely to experience if you are good at managing your emotions:

- Succeeding in education
- Experiencing better mental and physical health
- Feeling happier
- Achieving enhanced creativity
- Being more popular with others
- Enjoying stronger marriages and relationships
- Being more trusted
- Having fewer drinking problems and addictions

- Being less likely to commit crime
- Being less abusive
- Living longer
- Enjoying success in life

In short, if we can HAC our brain (manage our emotions) effectively, we become more resilient. This makes it easier to do important things really well. Remember, the first step of the HACing process is recognizing helpful and unhelpful behavior. We use Will Power to Self-Watch our thoughts and actions. Then, if we notice we are doing unhelpful things, we can also use our Will Power to deliberately begin switching our attention to more helpful things.

It is also important to say that Will Power is a limited resource, and this is why we need to use insights from behavioral science to build robust new habits. We will talk about habits, and how to develop more long-lasting helpful ones, in much greater detail a little bit later.

Right now, let's take a deep dive into our emotions and learn more about the role Will Power plays in emotional regulation.

14

THE "SECRET" SCIENCE OF FULFILLING YOUR POTENTIAL: EMOTIONAL REGULATION

WARNING! This short chapter is science heavy, but I will guide you through it and try to make it as easy as possible to understand. One of the big differences with Tougher Minds and the journey to becoming a Habit Mechanic is that cutting-edge science is the foundation of our work. If you understand the scientific underpinnings of the habit building techniques you learn in this book, they will be more powerful in helping you and those around you make lasting beneficial changes.

Here we go...

The scientific name I prefer to use to describe "HACing" (pronounced "hacking") is *emotional regulation*.

Effective emotional regulation underpins all aspects of wellbeing and high performance. Getting good at it is central to becoming a Habit Mechanic. Professor Barbara Fredrickson's work persuaded me that emotions are immediate biological signals that command us to act. This means emotions drive attention, and attention drives learning.

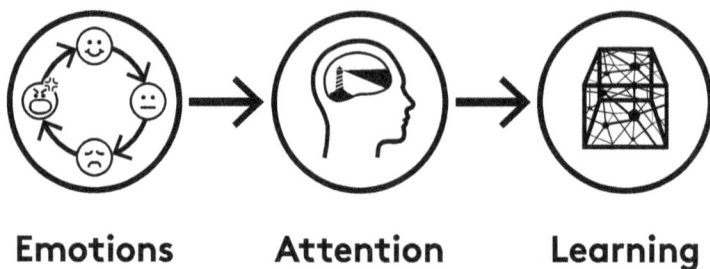

Emotions   Attention   Learning

Figure 14.1: Emotions demand your attention and therefore drive what you learn/get good at (for better or for worse).

Emotional regulation is the engine that drives your abilities to learn. If you want to win the Learning War, the first thing you need to focus your learning superpower on is improving emotional regulation.

Both helpful and unhelpful emotional regulation brain regions (see Figure 14.2) can be strengthened with practice. So, we can all learn how to get worse at regulating our emotions. The good news is you have already begun improving your emotional regulation skills and habits by using Habit Mechanic Tools (e.g., Daily TEA Plan, Daily 3:1 Reflection, APE Brain Test, etc.).

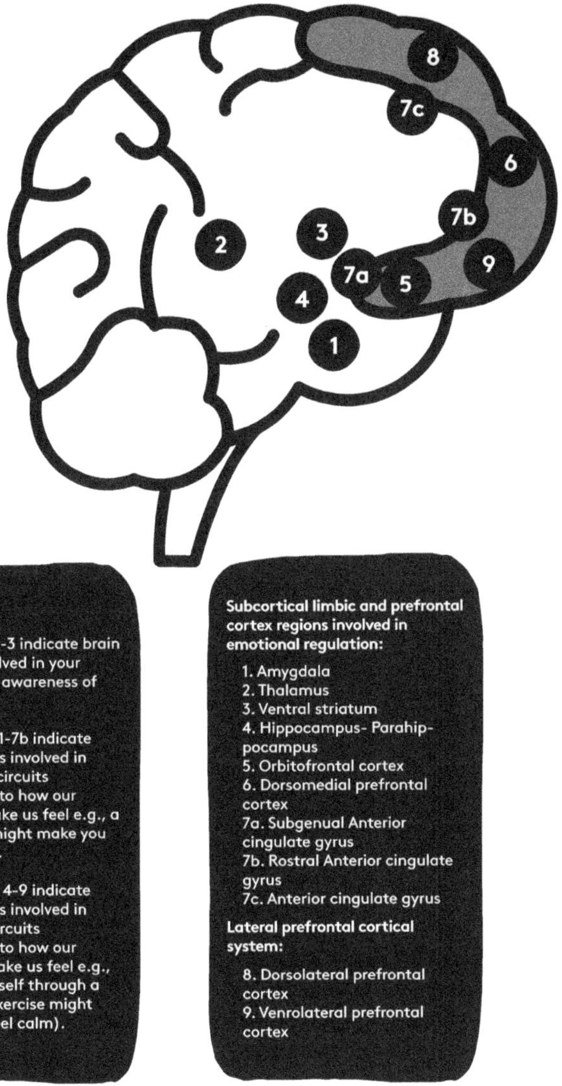

Key:

i. Numbers 1-3 indicate brain regions involved in your preconsious awareness of emotions.

ii. Numbers 1-7b indicate brain regions involved in bottom-up circuits (connected to how our instincts make us feel e.g., a loud bang might make you feel scared).

iii. Numbers 4-9 indicate brain regions involved in top-down circuits (connected to how our thoughts make us feel e.g., talking yourself through a breathing exercise might make you feel calm).

Subcortical limbic and prefrontal cortex regions involved in emotional regulation:

1. Amygdala
2. Thalamus
3. Ventral striatum
4. Hippocampus- Parahip-pocampus
5. Orbitofrontal cortex
6. Dorsomedial prefrontal cortex

7a. Subgenual Anterior cingulate gyrus
7b. Rostral Anterior cingulate gyrus
7c. Anterior cingulate gyrus

Lateral prefrontal cortical system:

8. Dorsolateral prefrontal cortex
9. Venrolateral prefrontal cortex

Figure 14.2: A cartoon of a neural map of emotional regulation systems (adapted from Phillips, Ladouceur, and Drevets 2008[4]). To learn how these brain circuits change with focused practice, check out Professor Richard Davidson's research and Dr. John Arden's work (I have studied with Dr. Arden).

[4] M. L. Phillips, C. D. Ladouceur, and W. C. Drevets, "A neural model of voluntary and automatic emotion regulation: implications for understanding the pathophysiology and neurodevelopment of bipolar disorder," *Molecular Psychiatry* 13, no. 9 (September 2008): 833–57.

FAST AND SLOW EMOTIONAL REGULATION

Insights about the specific neural circuitry involved in emotional regulation have revealed that emotional regulation operates on a continuum.

Conscious, effortful, and controlled regulation is at one end of this. This is called **explicit emotional regulation** (or slow).

On the other end of the continuum is unconscious, and possibly effortless, regulation. This is called **implicit emotional regulation** (or fast).

Both fast (or implicit) and slow (or explicit) systems work together to regulate emotions.

Most importantly, this means we can automate some elements of emotional regulation. Or, in other words, turn it into helpful habits.

Don't worry if this still feels intangible, because understanding the specifics of the science is not essential for learning how to get good at managing your emotions and becoming a Habit Mechanic.

We'll now consider emotional regulation in more practical terms.

PROACTIVELY MANAGE YOUR EMOTIONS

Emotions arise from a combination of your thoughts and feelings. The first step to managing your emotions is being more aware of them. We know HUE's (Horribly Unhelpful Emotions) first instinct is to use the lighthouse searchlight to seek out and dwell on threats and problems. But we are not always fully aware when and why this is happening, so negative emotional states can last for longer than necessary.

To deal with this more effectively, we can use Will Power to help us Self-Watch. For example, at the end of every day, we might take a few moments to think about our thoughts and feelings (emotions) and whether they are helping us be our best. If they are not, we can take action. Successfully regulating your emotions might take some time, but if you are proactive, you will do it faster and waste less time dwelling on unhelpful thoughts.

YOU CAN TAKE MORE RESPONSIBILITY
FOR MANAGING YOUR EMOTIONS

Kristina Vogel is a former record-breaking German cyclist. She won two gold medals and a bronze at the Olympic Games, and 11 world titles. She was a genuine global sports star and champion.

Unfortunately, at age 27, she suffered serious spinal and chest injuries in a training accident at her home velodrome in Cottbus, Germany. The incident in June 2018 left her paralyzed; Kristina will never walk again. In the aftermath of the accident, she explained her feelings in an article on the BBC Sport website.

"I realized quickly I would not walk again," she said.

"Tears will not help. It is what it is. I am ready to take on this challenge and make the best of it."

In a news conference at the Berlin hospital where she was treated, Vogel described to the BBC the moments following the crash.

"I said 'breathe, breathe, breathe' and then I checked," she said. "Then I saw where I lay, how I was. When my shoes were off, I knew that this was it with the walking.

"Asking 'why me?' does not bring you any further. I want to get back into life, not depend on a lot of help. I must use this strength I had in competitions for my life."

In 2019, Kristina Vogel gave a follow-up interview to the BBC. This was done by British cycling great Sir Chris Hoy.

In a supporting article on the BBC Sport website, Hoy wrote about Vogel's take on her situation. He explained how the German told him: "This is the toughest challenge ever, but what do you do? Lie in bed and do nothing each day? Or take it on and achieve what you can?" Kristina also said: "I am still happy to be here, and my situation could have been worse than it is…it could be that I have no movement in my arms."

Sir Chris also outlined how Kristina "talked about having new goals and new things you can look forward to in life. She talked about how lucky she felt to have support from all around the world to help get an adapted car, a new wheelchair and a new house that is going to be a bungalow with wider door frames and better access."

This is what we might call a world champion example of somebody taking responsibility for what they can control and regulating their emotions. In other words, doing their best to be their best.

Vogel successfully reappraised the meaning of her life-changing accident. She began to think about how things could have been worse and looked for benefits. She asked how she could adapt her personal goals. And she identified what sporting opportunities she still had.

Just like Kristina, you can also learn to think about your life circumstances in a much more helpful way.

HOW TO START REGULATING
YOUR EMOTIONS

There is another useful way of understanding your emotions. Psychologists use a tool known as the *Positive and Negative Affect Schedule (PANAS)* to help people monitor and measure their emotions and mood in a given situation. The PANAS emotions are shown in Figure 14.3.

I will use the PANAS emotions to explain an example emotional journey after a stressful experience, and show how we can take more control over our emotions than we imagine.

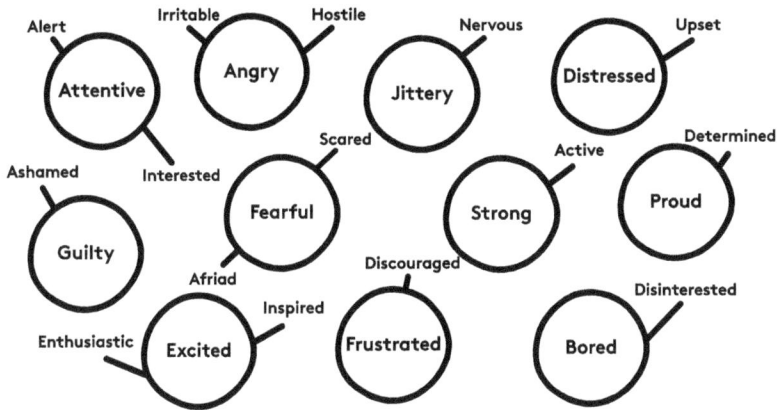

Figure 14.3. The PANAS emotions organized as main emotions and subcategory emotions—as detailed on the PANAS questionnaire.

AN EXAMPLE OF SUCCESSFUL EMOTIONAL REGULATION

Imagine going into a pay review meeting at work. You are very confident. You've been telling your friends and family you'll receive an increase. But in the meeting, you are told otherwise. There is a major disconnect between what you expected and what actually happened. HUE's natural response is to make you *angry*.

Then you might start to feel *guilty* for letting people down (no new house for your family—you were planning to move to a better school district). Then you get *fearful*. Will your family think you've let them down?

The above response is natural. If you think back to the Lighthouse Brain model, you will remember that HUE's first instinct is to dwell on threats and problems.

However, you can intervene.

Step 1. You can use your Will Power. First, you can use it to notice these unhelpful thoughts and feelings. This will shift your emotional focus from fear to being more **attentive** to the fact that you are dwelling on the negatives. By doing this, you are stepping back and using perspective, which makes refocusing and reframing your thoughts easier.

Step 2. Then you can use your Will Power to look for beneficial aspects in what has happened. For example, you now know what to do to get a pay raise next year. Or you can see that a different workplace is more suitable for you. You start to feel **excited** about the future. You realize you can make your family **proud** again after this setback. You start to feel much **stronger**.

This may happen over days or weeks. The key is to proactively manage your thoughts and deliberately pay attention to more helpful ones (I will show you how in Chapters 22 and 23). Doing this will help you manage your emotions and thinking and take more control over your life. This is the essence of successful emotional regulation and central to becoming a Habit Mechanic.

When we encounter a stressful situation, we cannot avoid feeling stressed. But Habit Mechanics recognize that they do have some level of control over their emotional states, and they definitely have more control over them than anybody else. Me Power Conditioning (deliberately working toward being our best) empowers us to do our best to be our best. Habit Mechanics take responsibility for doing this.

Proactively shifting your attention from unhelpful to helpful thoughts will save you time. Instead of spending weeks dwelling, you could deal with negative emotions in a day... an hour... or even minutes. This makes it much easier to achieve your health, happiness, and performance goals.

If it is helpful, take a moment to make a few notes about, or think about, how good you are at noticing and managing your unhelpful emotions.

If you manage people, take a moment to make a few notes about, or think about, how good they are at noticing and managing their unhelpful emotions.

HOW WILL IMPROVING MY EMOTIONAL
REGULATION MAKE ME HAPPIER?

What is happiness?

My understanding of what it means to be happy is drawn from two broad schools of thought.

One is called the **hedonic approach**. This focuses on achieving a state of happiness—via experiencing positive emotions—by pursuing pleasure (doing things that make you feel good in the short-term) and avoiding pain, boredom, and stress.

The other is called the **eudemonic approach**. This focuses on delaying short-term gratification in pursuit of bigger, more meaningful goals. This sometimes means experiencing negative but helpful emotions, for example, pain, boredom, and stress. This could mean, for example, resisting the desire to check your phone so you can focus on writing your book; defying HUE's desire to watch the next episode of your favorite TV show so you can get to bed on time; and making yourself do your daily, weekly, and monthly planning and reflection exercises even though it is not always that enjoyable and there are other things your HUE would prefer to do.

For simplicity, we will refer to the hedonic approach as **pleasure**, and to the eudemonic approach as **Habit Mechanic development**.

To achieve happiness, first we need our brain to be working well. There-fore, we need good sleep, diet, and exercise habits (we will cover this in

Chapter 19), and to have positive personal relationships (think of the "P"/ Perceived in APE).

Then we need to strike a balance of both pleasure and Habit Mechanic development.

Why Is Striking This Balance Difficult?

HUE can have a profoundly negative impact on how engaged, fulfilled, and satisfied you feel with life. The problem is that the activities we engage in to pursue pleasure (the hedonic part of the happiness equation) can be very rewarding for HUE, meaning that we can become addicted to them, and they become unhelpful habits. By addiction I mean that we continue to engage in behaviors even though they are having negative consequences on our health, happiness, and being our best. For example, you know that checking your phone as regularly as you do is not good for you, but you can't stop yourself.

The trouble is that the states of pleasure we derive from these experiences disappear quickly, and our happiness returns to levels it was at prior to the experience, or worse still even lower.

So, wanting to feel good (pleasure) all the time is leading to lots of people feeling happy for short periods but deeply unsatisfied for most of the time.

Also, wanting to feel good (pleasure) all the time is not always compatible with great sleep, diet, and exercise habits, and great relationships with other people.

What Will Make You Happier?

To sustain feelings of happiness, we must also challenge ourselves to grow by becoming Habit Mechanics. This means that we will experience the highs and lows of pushing ourselves to our limits. We will expose our weaknesses but also discover our strengths. People who engage in this type of purposeful development experience flourishing and higher levels of wellbeing.

The challenge is that HUE is incentivized to do things that help you stay alive, focus on what important people think about you, and conserve energy. So pushing and challenging ourselves to grow can be difficult because not all of the work you will do to become a Habit Mechanic will give you immediate gratification. You will have to expose your weaknesses and fail from time to time. None of these ideas are appealing to HUE, so it resists.

Is Being Unhappy Addictive?

HUE can become addicted to pursuing pleasure (hedonic states). And it can compel you to avoid Habit Mechanic development activities (eudemonia). This is because challenging yourself to do better can expose your weaknesses. So HUE talks you out of engaging in challenging developmental processes, or talks you into giving up, and then beats you up for failing or not trying at all. So pursuing happiness is one thing, but achieving a good balance of pleasure and Habit Mechanic development is another.

I believe the best way to strike a pleasure/Habit Mechanic development balance is by developing our emotional regulation skills and habits (in other words, becoming a Habit Mechanic). This makes managing HUE and becoming truly happy much easier.

HOW CAN I IMPROVE MY
EMOTIONAL REGULATION SKILLS?

For the remainder of the book, I am going to show you how to strengthen your abilities to regulate your emotions. I will do this by showing you how to analyze your habits and build more helpful ones for improved

- work-life balance;
- Habit Mechanic intelligence;
- motivation;
- stress management;
- sleep, diet, and exercise;
- confidence;
- performance under pressure;
- focus and productivity; and
- leadership.

Do You Want to Practice Regulating Your Emotions Right Now?

Use the Daily TEA Plan or the Daily 3:1 Reflection I introduced earlier.

To learn more simple and practical emotional regulation tools, keep reading. I call these Habit Mechanic Tools.

I think of Habit Mechanic Tools like bicycle stabilizers. They are designed to help you learn how to become a Habit Mechanic. The more skilled you become, and the more helpful habits you develop, the less reliant you will be on your Habit Mechanic Tools. But the tools will always be there to fall back on when you notice your habits slipping and during the more challenging periods of your life.

Congratulations! You have now completed Step 2!

Before you move on to Step 3, please take a moment to notice (in the Habit Mechanic language and tools list) everything you have learned so far. You are doing great!

HABIT MECHANIC LANGUAGE AND
TOOLS COVERED IN STEP 2...

Core Language

Lighthouse Brain—A simple model to help you understand the gist of how your brain works so you can begin to improve your thinking. (Chapter 10) ☑

HUE (Horribly Unhelpful Emotions)—An imaginary character who lives in your brain who can make you worry and make it difficult for you to be your best. (Chapter 10) ☑

Willomenia Power or Will Power—An imaginary character who lives in your brain who can help you manage HUE. (Chapter 10) ☑

APE (Alive Perceived Energy) Brain—An easy acronym to help you understand your survival brain/limbic regions of the brain. (Chapter 11) ☑

HAC (Helpful Attention Control) Brain—An easy acronym to help you understand your prefrontal cortex. (Chapter 11) ☑

Self-Watching—Reflecting and thinking about yourself in a focused and systematic way. (Chapter 12) ☑

Me Power Wish List—A list of all the small new helpful habits you would like to build. (Chapter 12) ☑

Hedonism (pleasure)—This focuses on seeking short-term gratification and immediate rewards. (Chapter 14) ☑

Eudemonia (Habit Mechanic development)—This focuses on delaying short-term gratification, and sometimes enduring pain, boredom, and stress in order to develop yourself, grow, and achieve big meaningful goals. (Chapter 14) ☑

Self-Reflection Tools

APE Brain Test—A quick Self-Watching exercise to help you reflect on your helpful and unhelpful habits. (Chapter 12) ☑

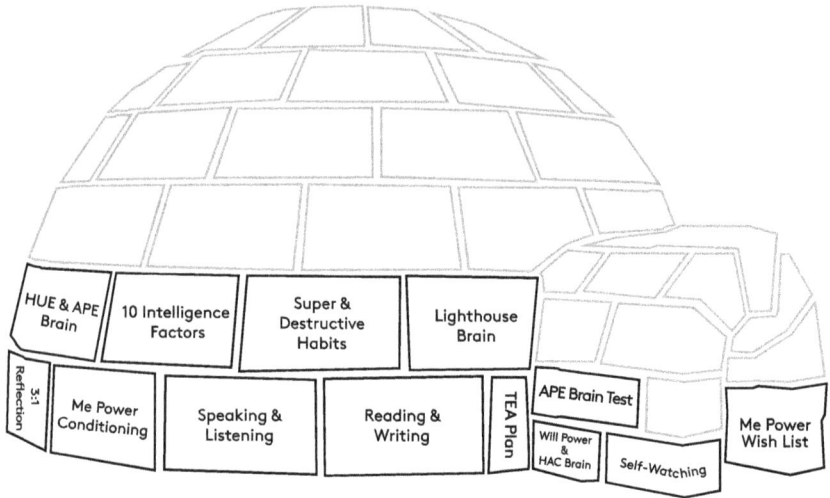

Figure 14.4: Your Habit Mechanic intelligence igloo is building up!

APPENDIX B

HOW ACTIVATION LEVELS CONNECT TO BRAIN STATES

While the main text focuses on the three key Brain States (High Charge, Medium Charge, and Recharge), this appendix explores the deeper science of how these states actually work through the concept of Activation Levels. Drawing from The Habit Mechanic, this detailed exploration helps explain why matching tasks to Brain States is so crucial in the AI era, and how to consciously manage your mental energy throughout the day.

Understanding Activation Levels provides the scientific foundation for why Brain State optimization is so powerful. Just as the New Zealand All Blacks learned to manage their mental states for peak performance through their 'blue head' versus 'red head' system, professionals in the AI era need to understand and control their Activation Levels to make the most of both their natural capabilities and AI tools.

21

CONTROL YOUR ACTIVATION LEVELS TO FEEL BETTER AND MAKE EVERYTHING YOU DO EASIER

The New Zealand All Blacks are arguably one of the most successful sporting teams in human history. They are the only team with an overall winning record against every other country in the world. Their win rate over 100 years is around 77 percent. In recent history, it is 80 percent. And, in October 2015, they became the first team to win back-to-back Rugby World Cups.

In both the build-up and aftermath of that tournament, much press coverage highlighted how the All Blacks drew on collective and individual mental resilience to help them prevail in the face of on-field setbacks and challenges.

These high levels of resilience were not an accident, but something the All Blacks purposefully developed through a deliberate process of acquiring key mental skills. This was undertaken in the noughties (the decade from

2000 to 2009) as a response to several high-profile defeats that appeared to be the result of choking under pressure.

The All Blacks sought to develop a culture that focused on individual character and outstanding leadership. One of their mantras was "Better People Make Better All Blacks." A central pillar of their on-field performance approach was to "keep a blue head," that is, an optimal performance state, and avoid often unhelpful and panicky "red head" states. I think of this as an All Black intelligent Self-Watching process. You can learn how to use a similar approach to manage what I call "Activation."

In this chapter, I'm going to introduce the concept of Activation, and also show you how to proactively manage your "Activation levels."

THE POWER OF ACTIVATION

Another way to describe the All Blacks' blue and red head states is Activation. Being able to manage your mental and physical Activation is essential if you want to be your best and fulfill your potential.

Activation is a concept I've developed to make it easier for people to better manage their sleep, relaxation/downtime, focus, and stress levels.

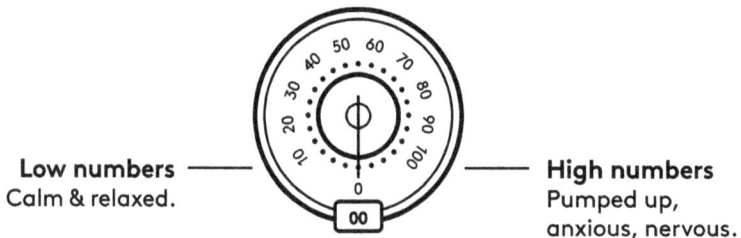

Low numbers
Calm & relaxed.

High numbers
Pumped up,
anxious, nervous.

*Figure 21.1: A simple overview of the Activation scale,
or sometimes I refer to it as the Activation dial.*

Optimizing diet, exercise, and sleep (DES) habits will be the foundations for your health, happiness, and success. But building better "Activation management" habits comes a close second. All four are interconnected. Achieving the correct Activation levels can make DES habits easier to build. And building better DES habits can make it easier to achieve optimal Activation levels.

Activation management is essential for building more helpful habits in all the areas I have discussed:

- Improving diet, exercise, and sleep for better brain performance
- Better stress management
- Spending less time thinking unhelpful thoughts
- Being focused to drive productivity, creativity, and problem-solving
- Building and maintaining robust levels of confidence
- Performing well under pressure
- Better leadership for improved individual and team performance

All make it easier to manage work-life balance.

WHAT DO WE MEAN BY "ACTIVATION"?

Imagine a scale that runs from zero all the way to 100.

Only those who are no longer with us are at zero on the Activation scale. Low numbers represent feeling sleepy, calm, and relaxed. High numbers represent being excited, pumped up, or nervous. If your heart is beating as fast as it can, you'd be at 100 on the Activation scale.

Activation Scale

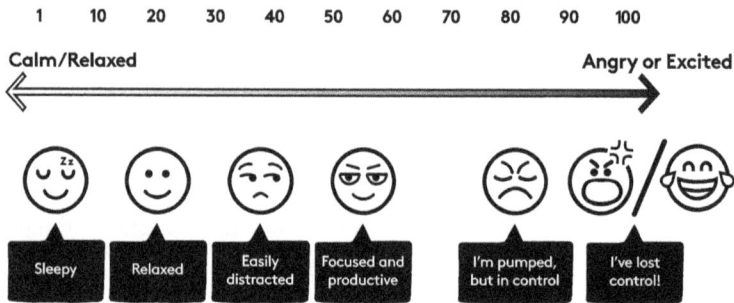

Figure 21.2: A more in-depth insight into different Activation levels. These are my personal examples.

Understanding your ideal Activation level for different tasks and activities, and having the knowledge and skills to control your Activation, is a core ingredient of health, happiness, and performance (imagine trying to sleep if you were at 100!).

HOW TO TAKE CONTROL OF YOUR BRAIN STATES

We can directly connect our three Brain States—introduced in the main text—to these Activation levels. Each state requires a different optimal range on the Activation scale to function effectively. Let me illustrate this using my own patterns:

For Recharge—I need to achieve specific levels depending on the type of recovery needed:

- Between 1 and 5 for quality sleep
- Between 10 and 20 for Non-sleep Recharge activities like meditation or quiet reflection

For **Medium Charge**—the state where I handle routine tasks efficiently—I need to maintain levels between 30 and 50. This provides enough energy for consistent performance without draining my resources.

For **High Charge**—when I need my most sophisticated thinking capabilities—I aim for levels between 55 and 60. This range gives me optimal cognitive performance without tipping into stress or overwhelm.

Take a moment to reflect on your own ideal Activation levels for each Brain State. Remember, these are starting points that you can adjust as you learn more about your own patterns:

Recharge (sleep) level: _____   Non-sleep Recharge: _____
Medium Charge level: _____   High Charge level: _____

The key to optimizing your Brain States lies in matching your activities to these appropriate Activation levels. Consider two common scenarios that illustrate why this matching is so crucial:

1. If you arrive at the office early to tackle complex strategic work—an activity requiring your High Charge state—but your Activation level is extremely low due to poor sleep, you'll struggle to perform effectively. Your brain simply isn't in the right state for sophisticated thinking.

2. Conversely, if you're trying to achieve quality sleep—requiring your deepest Recharge state - but you've just read a challenging work email that has pushed your Activation level high, you'll find it nearly impossible to drift off. Your brain is too energized for proper recovery.

Now that you understand how Brain States and Activation levels connect, I encourage you to review and update your Optimal Activation Review (detailed later in this chapter). This will help you create more precise strategies for managing your energy throughout the day.

THINKING ABOUT YOUR IDEAL ACTIVATION LEVELS

A simple Self-Watching exercise can help you learn more about your daily Activation levels. Remember, Self-Watching is the first stage of a SWAP (Self-Watching, Aim, Plan).

Don't worry if you are not 100 percent certain of your answers. If you are unsure, go with your gut. The more you think about your Activation, the more you will learn which Activation levels work best for you.

First, write down the Activation level (number) you think you are at right now. _____

Next, if you can, stand up. Then, if you can, jump up and down on the spot for 5 or 10 seconds. Now, write your new Activation level. _____

Tip: Getting up and moving around can quickly increase your Activation level.

Next, write down the ideal Activation level you think you need to achieve to fall into a deep sleep tonight (e.g., 1). _____

Next, think about how easy you find it to achieve the correct sleeping Activation level. Rank this from 1 (difficult) to 10 (easy). _____ /10

To perform well at work, you need to achieve a certain Activation level. On average, people feel they need to be around 50 on the scale to work efficiently and effectively. I call this the "Ideal Work" Activation level.

Write down your Ideal Work Activation level (e.g., 55). _____

How easy is it for you to consistently achieve the correct Ideal Work Activation level? Rank this from 1 (difficult) to 10 (easy). _____ /10

Reflect?

If it is helpful, write down a few notes on what you have learned about your Activation levels.

LEARNING MORE ABOUT YOUR OPTIMAL ACTIVATION

Different Activation Levels to Boost Your Learning

Activation can positively or negatively impact many other areas of your life. Have you ever been trying to read a complicated report and it feels like the words are bouncing off your eyes, and that nothing will go into your brain?

Part of the problem here is that your Activation level is incorrect. Alertness is the first part of concentration—if you are not alert, it will be harder to learn the information in a complicated report. So, the first step to maximizing your focus, learning, and performance on a given task is understanding which Activation level is ideal for that task.

Write down the ideal Activation level (number) YOU think you need to be at to successfully complete a difficult piece of reading. For me, it is 60. _____

It is highly likely that your Ideal Work Activation level has a range, and different learning tasks, at different times of the day, might require slightly different ideal Activation levels. It is important to be aware of your ideal Activation levels (for different tasks and activities) to give yourself the best chance of achieving that correct level—whether for the first task in the morning, at lunch, or at the end of the day. I will explore this in more detail in Chapter 25, where I will explain Brain States in more detail, and show you how to create a "Will Power Story" to optimize your focus each day.

Different Activation Levels to Boost Your Performance

Activation can also be used as a performance skill. For example, to deliver an excellent presentation you need to achieve a certain Activation level (e.g., 65).

According to reports, New Zealand rugby players consciously managed their Activation during training and matches. Rugby is a physical sport, and certain skills require high Activation to perform them well. For example, making a successful rugby tackle requires high Activation—say an 85. But if your Activation is too high (99), you might give away a penalty.

However, other actions in rugby—such as taking a successful penalty kick—require much lower Activation—maybe a 50.

So different activities have different ideal Activation levels. You might have to switch between these to optimize your performance.

Relaxation Activation Levels

As well as considering ideal Activation levels for learning and performance, we should also think about ideal levels for relaxation (e.g., taking a break and switching off). Sleep is the ultimate way to recharge your brain, but you also need to use relaxation activities for the same purpose. I call these activities "Non-Sleep Recharge."

Research shows many of us do not make optimal use of relaxation and downtime. Our brains are not recharging properly during these periods. After a break, you should feel refreshed and recharged. Yet many of us feel more tired than we did before.

One of the challenges here is HUE (Horribly Unhelpful Emotions). It is on a constant search for threats and problems or new, exciting, fun things that make us feel good. These activities require higher levels of Activation than are helpful when we are trying to recharge our brains (e.g., spending breaks on our smartphones or social media or worrying about things we cannot control is not a good way to recharge our brains).

Think about the ideal Activation level you should be trying to achieve during breaks and downtime to help you quiet your mind and recharge your brain (e.g., at break times I Aim to reduce my Activation level to a 20). Think of this as your Optimal Non-Sleep Recharge Activation level.

Write down your Optimal Non-Sleep Recharge Activation level: _____

HOW CAN I MANAGE MY ACTIVATION LEVELS?

Self-Watching and recognizing which Activation levels YOU need to achieve (your Aim) during different tasks, performances, and times of the day is the first step to successful Activation management. But you also need Plans to make your ideal Activation levels a reality.

To help you make better Plans, we are going to explore the brain science behind Activation management. We will begin by introducing the brain chemistry connected to Activation.

Getting the Basics Right—Activation Science

Brain activity is generated partly by electric impulses and partly by chemical messengers called neurotransmitters. Some of your neurotransmitters can help you manage your Activation.

Glutamate and GABA are two important neurotransmitters in relation to Activation. Glutamate excites the brain, and GABA slows down activity. Many scientists also recognize three other types of neurotransmitters as being particularly important:

Serotonin helps keep brain activity under control and helps you reduce Activation levels.

Noradrenaline or **Norepinephrine** is essential for achieving the type of Activation levels you need for focused work, study, and practice.

Dopamine allows you to sharpen and focus your attention onto the things you need to learn. Best known for making you feel good, it also acts like a save button for the brain, making it essential for learning new information.

Successfully managing DES (diet, exercise, sleep) is key to giving your brain, and therefore your brain chemistry, the best chance of working properly. That's why I ask you to focus on developing good daily DES habits, because it makes managing your Activation levels easier.

Now that we've covered the basics, let's think about some specific techniques and tools you can use in your Activation management Plans.

Breathing Management

Breathing management is the most powerful technique you can use to both increase and decrease Activation.

Increased Activation is strongly connected to what is commonly called the fight or flight (or freeze) response. This is driven by a reaction in our brain's HPA (hypothalamic-pituitary-adrenal) axis when we experience a stress response.

In the 1970s, Professor Herbert Benson from Harvard University wrote *The Relaxation Response* about successfully managing the fight/flight response.

Benson showed that breathing is the fight/flight factor we have the most control over. By reducing our breathing rates, we can also reduce our heart rate, blood pressure, metabolism, muscle tension, and mental arousal. So **Activation can be lowered by reducing breathing rates**.

Equally, when we increase our breathing rate, our heart rate, blood pressure, metabolism, muscle tension, and mental arousal also increase.

So, **Activation can be increased by breathing faster** or by doing activities that cause you to breathe faster.

To master breathing control, you need to understand how thinking works. Imagine that your thoughts have two different but connected parts: self-talk and mental imagery.

Controlling Your Thoughts

To understand this, let's think about how the All Blacks controlled their Activation during a game. Former All Black Brad Thorn is one of the most successful rugby players of all time. He won 20 major titles, including a World Cup, in a 22-year career.

In an article for the *Independent* newspaper, Brian Ashton (former England rugby union coach) reported that Graham Henry (the then head coach of the All Blacks) had disclosed Brad Thorn's very practical trigger for cooling down his emotions. He poured a bottle of water over himself. This helped him move himself from an unhelpful "red head" state (e.g., approximately 90–100 on the Activation dial) during a game to a more helpful "blue head" state (e.g., approximately 50–80 on the Activation dial).

Often in sport, people talk about having fire in your belly and ice in your veins and head—and not letting the fire melt the ice. This was Thorn's way of making sure his fire did not melt his ice.

What Can We Learn from This?

First, it is important to recognize that Thorn made a conscious decision to pour the water over his head and face to help him achieve a more helpful thinking state. So, this is an example of Brad Thorn deliberately HACing (hacking) his brain (or regulating his emotions).

To understand what Thorn might have been thinking, and what we can learn from this, let's dig deeper into "self-talk," or the words we say in our heads.

Self-Talk and Focus Words

To prompt ourselves to do things, we talk to ourselves: "I need to finish this report by tomorrow." "I am so tired; I need to get an early night." "That donut looks so good; it will taste amazing, and I need to have it!" "I am getting angry so I will pour some water over my head and face to help me calm down." 😊

You are talking to yourself right now as you read these words. Previously we used the example of wearing an invisible pair of headphones to illustrate this point.

Gaining control over your self-talk is vital if you want to gain control over Activation. When we deliberately use words to help us think more effectively,

I call them "Focus Words." For example, telling yourself to "Focus" and "Get on with it" can help increase your Activation. Telling yourself to "Focus on my breathing and slow it down" can help you reduce your Activation and relax.

If you don't have control over your self-talk, you might be telling yourself things that have a negative impact on your Activation—for example, "I am nervous," "I am useless," or lying in bed at night telling yourself how terrible tomorrow will be if you don't get a good night sleep. These examples will not help you control your Activation and will trigger a stress response (we will dig deeper into "the stress response" in Chapter 22). The good news is you can learn how to get better at controlling your self-talk with practice, and I will show you how later.

Mental Imagery and Focus Pictures

As well as self-talk, we also think in pictures or mental imagery. Mental imagery is an important part of your thought process. You constantly use it.

For example, picture, in your mind's eye, your home's front door. Without having any visual stimulus, you can see a picture *in* your mind's eye.

Visually, you are constantly switching between what you can see through your eyes (e.g., this book) and what you can see in your mind's eye.

When we deliberately use pictures to help us think more effectively, I call them "Focus Pictures." For example, picturing the Activation dial (in your mind's eye) getting lower and lower as you deliberately slow down your breathing can help you reduce your Activation level. Imagining the Activation dial increasing can help you increase your Activation level. Equally, you could imagine yourself lying on a peaceful beach to help you relax, or imagine a person who has upset you in the past to pump yourself up.

If you don't have control over the pictures in your mind's eye, you might be seeing the worst-case scenario unfolding. This will not help you control your Activation. The good news is you can learn how to get better at controlling your mental imagery with practice, and I will show you how later.

Brad Thorn's Self-Talk and Mental Imagery

When Brad Thorn was pouring water over himself, I do not know exactly what he was thinking. But I do know his thoughts were likely a combination of both self-talk (or Focus Words) and mental imagery (or Focus Pictures). So below I have mapped out a hypothetical example of his thinking process. This is designed to help you understand how you can better use Focus Words and Pictures to manage your Activation.

First Thorn had to do some intelligent **Self-Watching**: he noticed he was not at the correct Activation level. This would have involved him talking to himself: "You need to get out of the red head zone and into the blue head zone."

As he did this, he might have also pictured the Activation dial in his mind's eye and noticed it was too high.

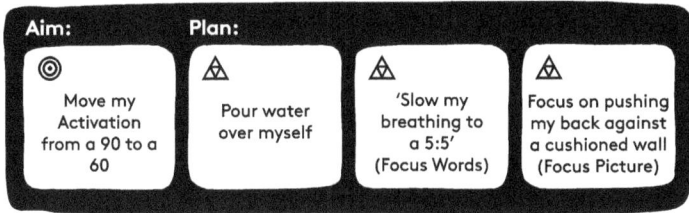

Aim:	**Plan:**		
◎	⚠	⚠	⚠
Move my Activation from a 90 to a 60	Pour water over myself	'Slow my breathing to a 5:5' (Focus Words)	Focus on pushing my back against a cushioned wall (Focus Picture)

Figure 21.3: Brad Thorn's hypothetical Aim and Plan.

Next, he might have set an **Aim**. He might have said to himself, "I need to move down from a 90 to a 60." So achieving an Activation level of 60 was his Aim.

Finally, to change his Activation he needed a **Plan**. The first part of his Plan was getting a bottle of water and pouring it over himself.

The second part of his Plan—which was triggered by pouring water over his head and face—might have been to control his breathing.

He might have used a relaxation technique called "centering," which is designed to begin and manage the Relaxation Response by reducing breathing rates and body tension. This is achieved by first standing or sitting in a comfortable position with your body weight equally distributed between the left and right sides of your body.

Brad Thorn was standing, and to achieve a centered position he might have imagined (a Focus Picture) that he was pushing his back flat against a soft cushioned wall, making sure that his legs were straight and flat against this wall. Next, he might have used self-talk (Focus Words) to focus on slowing his breathing pattern down to what I call a 5:5—talking himself through the process of breathing out for five seconds and then breathing in for five seconds, and repeating this pattern.

He might have told himself to inhale through his nose and draw the air down into his stomach. He might have used words such as "loose" and "relax" to help release some of the tension in his neck and shoulder muscles. Finally, he might have pictured the Activation dial in his mind's eye, and focused on moving the dial down from a 90 to a 60 as he exhaled.

This might have all happened within a period of 60 seconds. And because Brad Thorn had spent time practicing his Activation management, moving it from knowledge-to-skill-to-habit, it was a reasonably effortless process for him.

I know that pouring a bottle of water over your head is not that practical when sitting at your desk, so don't feel you have to follow this example step by step 😊. I will show you how to apply these ideas in your day-to-day life shortly.

Reflect?

If it is helpful, write down a few notes about what you have learned about using breathing, and Focus Words and Pictures, to manage your Activation.

ACTIVATION MANAGEMENT HABITS

We can think about my description of Brad Thorn's Activation management within the TRAIT Habit Loop.

The **Trigger** is him recognizing his red head state.

His **Routine** used self-talk and mental imagery to slow his breathing, relax his body, and pour cold water over his head and face.

The **APE** (Alive, Perceived, Energy) **Incentive** was that this routine would help him perform better and reap all the associated rewards—like winning the Rugby World Cup.

Finally, the **Training** effect was the more Brad Thorn practiced this routine, the easier it became.

In the context of the Lighthouse Brain, we can imagine Brad Thorn was using this technique to help Will Power get HUE's attention onto what was most helpful. The more Thorn practiced, the more automatic it became for Will Power to help HUE pay attention to helpful thoughts.

The Brad Thorn example demonstrates the importance of breathing management, self-talk, and imagery in successful Activation management.

HOW TO SELF-WATCH YOUR ACTIVATION
DURING THE DAY

To help you effectively match your daily tasks and activities to the correct Activation levels, I have created a Habit Mechanic Tool called the "Optimal Activation Review."

Optimal Activation Review

Use the graph below to plot and compare your normal and optimal Activation levels.

Focus on your Activation throughout a working day.

Key
0 - Normal Activation Level
X - Optimal Activation Level

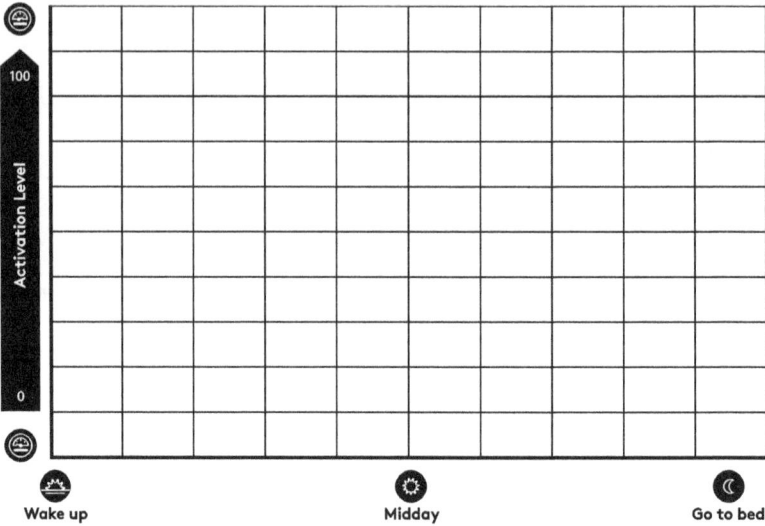

Figure 21.4: A blank Optimal Activation Review template.

You can use the Optimal Activation Review to track and compare normal and optimal Activation levels throughout a working day. If you work in the office some days, and from home on other days, you might want to create a separate profile for each situation.

This is a very visual process. To download the Optimal Activation Review PDF, go to tougherminds.co.uk/habitmechanic and click on "Resources" to get your copy.

Once you have downloaded it, take time to complete it.

Completing Your Optimal Activation Review

This tool will help you learn more about your Optimal Activation. The horizontal scale represents one day—from waking in the morning to going to bed in the evening. The vertical scale shows your Activation level from 0 to 100.

I have used a personal example to help you understand how the Optimal Activation Review tool helped me improve my Activation management. First, I plotted "Os" to show my normal Activation profile.

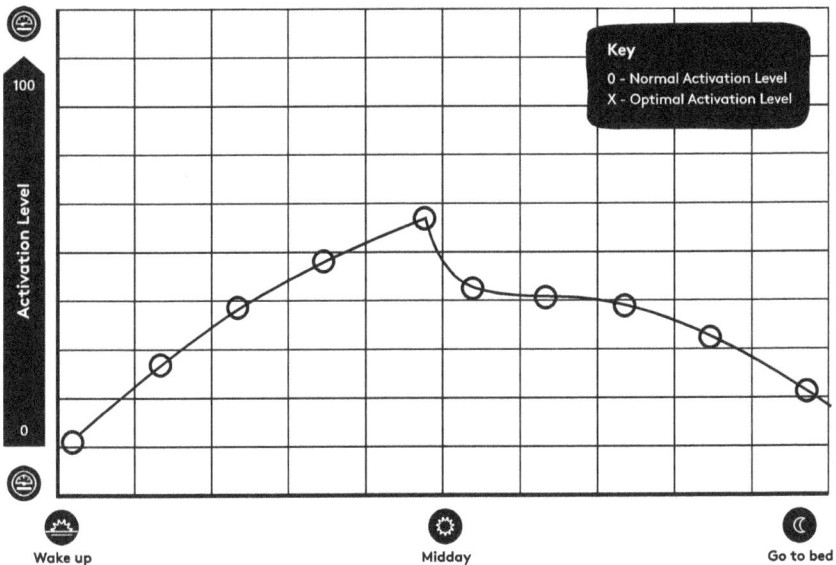

Figure 21.5: Optimal Activation Review showing my normal (now my old) Activation profile.

Before I improved my Activation management, I woke in the morning and my Activation level gradually rose as midday approached. It reached approximately 60 on the scale. But then it fell relatively quickly after lunch, which did not feel ideal.

Once I'd plotted my normal Activation profile, I then used crosses (Xs) to plot my ideal (or optimal) Activation levels throughout the course of a day.

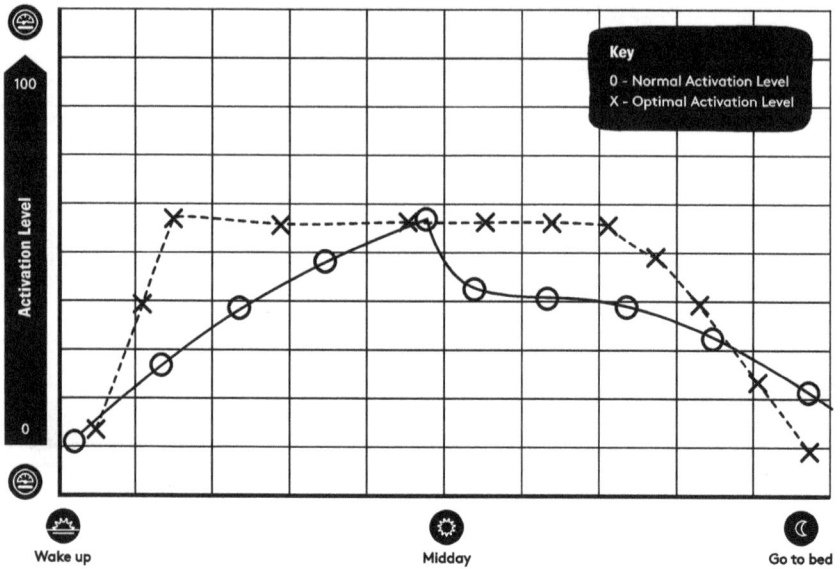

Figure 21.6: Optimal Activation Review showing my normal (but now old) Activation profile (Os) and my ideal (now my current) Activation profile (Xs).

By doing this, I was able to identify my biggest Activation challenges throughout the course of the day (which were in the morning and after lunch) and improve my Activation management. I will explain exactly how I did this in Chapter 25 when I show you how to create a daily "Will Power Story." But now I will share some specific Activation management skills you can begin using immediately.

HOW TO IMPROVE
NIGHTTIME ACTIVATION MANAGEMENT

Now that you have identified your biggest daily Activation challenges, let's dig deeper into Activation management improvement skills. We will build on the breathing management and Focus Words and Pictures skills I have already introduced.

Let's start with sleep. When you want to sleep, you need to lower your Activation levels. Think about the sleep elevator metaphor from earlier in this book (Chapter 19), where sleep has five levels and you move between them like an elevator does between five floors in a building.

You start at Level 5 (awake) and slowly move down to Level 1 (slow-wave sleep), then back up to Level 4, and so on. As you sleep, you move up and down in your sleep elevator, and it is natural to arrive back at Level 5 (awake) in the night.

Let's think about how you can reduce your Activation to secure better quality sleep.

STOP Your Technology Unintentionally Increasing Your Activation Levels!

To bring down your Activation levels low enough to fall asleep, you need sufficient levels of a sleeping hormone called melatonin to be present in your brain. Melatonin production is controlled by light. During daylight hours, your melatonin production is low. And using a hand-held screen that produces light, like a smartphone, tablet, or laptop, also reduces melatonin levels.

As well as reducing melatonin levels, the information you see on your devices might be exciting. This increases neurotransmitters like noradrenaline and dopamine. Or it might be stressful and increase hormones associated with the fight/flight response, like cortisol. Either way, it is not helping you achieve your ideal sleeping Activation level.

So the first step to achieving your sleep Activation level is to turn off technology one hour before you go to bed, and don't use it in bed.

Use Warm Water

You can use warm water (e.g., take a bath or shower) to help you reduce Activation levels before bed. We now understand that a reduction in body temperature is a trigger for sleep. Your body cools when you get out of the warm water, helping lower Activation levels and trigger sleep.

Use Focus Words and Pictures

Another technique you can use to decrease Activation levels at bedtime relates to Focus Words and Pictures. One example of using this technique to directly reduce Activation is imagining the Activation dial in your mind's eye—a Focus Picture—and at the same time use Focus Words to help you slow your breathing pattern. You might want to create a 4:7 breathing pattern (or whatever works best for you), telling yourself to breathe in slowly for four seconds—feeling your stomach expanding like a balloon—and breathe out slowly for seven seconds—feeling your shoulders and your neck relax. As you are doing this, you might see the Activation dial in your mind's eye getting lower and lower. You might repeat this until you achieve the desired Activation level. Do some personal research to learn which breathing pattern works best for you.

An example of a less direct way of using Focus Words and Pictures to reduce Activation is focusing on recalling a holiday that provided lasting positive memories. The Focus Words are you talking yourself through what happened on the holiday from start to finish, and the Focus Pictures are you seeing the holiday unfold—like you were watching a movie of it. You could use a similar approach, but instead focus on going on one of your favorite walks.

Other things can help lower your Activation levels:

- Making sure your bedroom is cool, quiet, and dark
- Being mindful of your daily caffeine intake
- Drinking enough water during the day to prevent dehydration
- Learning to relax your muscles with a routine called *progressive muscular relaxation*

Progressive Muscular Relaxation

This is a relaxation technique that can be used directly before you go to sleep, or while you are in bed. The aim is to systematically relax different muscles in the body. For example, you might start with the muscle groups in your feet and work up to your neck and head.

You focus on relaxing one muscle group at a time by learning to deliberately contract and relax muscles until all tension in that muscle group has disappeared. Self-talk (Focus Words) and imagery (Focus Pictures) are very important here. To learn how to do this, you can start with your right hand. Using self-talk, tell yourself to clench and squeeze your hand into a fist. Then tell yourself to open your hand and relax it—imagine it is as light as a feather. Once your hand feels relaxed, you can move onto your right forearm, again telling yourself to tense it as tightly as you can, and then relaxing it, and so on. So progressively, and systematically, you target different muscle groups in your body until all feel relaxed, and you have lowered your Activation level.

Reflect?

If it is helpful, write down a few notes about what you have learned about lowering your Activation levels before you go to bed.

HOW TO IMPROVE
DAYTIME ACTIVATION MANAGEMENT

If you are achieving good sleep Activation levels and therefore sleeping well, it will be much easier to control your Activation during the morning. So let's imagine you are struggling to achieve ideal Activation levels after lunch.

You might recognize your post-lunch Activation is typically at 40 when you would ideally like it to be 60. So you set an Aim to improve your score to a 60 more regularly.

Here are some Activation management techniques you could use in a Plan to increase your post-lunch Activation levels:

Food

Consider how the food you eat for lunch can impact your afternoon Activation. One way to categorize food is with the Glycemic Index (GI), which measures the speed at which food that contains carbohydrates increase your blood sugar levels. Foods that score high on the glycemic index are known as high GI. Foods with low GI contain sugars that enter the bloodstream slowly.

High GI food, like white bread, white rice, potatoes, chocolate bars, and sugary drinks, can give you an initial spike in your Activation levels, but then quickly reduce your Activation levels so you feel tired and sluggish.

Low GI food, like whole grain bread, nuts, and some fruits and some vegetables, allow you to maintain a more constant Activation level by releasing sugar into your blood more slowly.

Visit the NHS (or USDA) website for a helpful overview of GI foods.

Exercise

Exercise after lunch will also boost your Activation. Whether you take a short walk or do something more intense like going to the gym, it will help boost essential Activation-increasing brain chemicals like dopamine and BDNF, which will then enhance your focus in the afternoon.

Self-Talk and Mental Imagery

Another technique you can use to increase Activation levels is to use self-talk and mental imagery, just like we discussed in your sleep routine.

Imagine in your mind's eye the Activation dial getting higher (Focus Picture). At the same time, use self-talk (Focus Words) to help you increase your breathing pattern. Using a physical trigger like standing up and clenching your fist might also help. With practice, you will find a strategy that works to help you quickly increase your Activation. This should be a short, sharp—and if you are working in an office with others, quiet—technique 😄.

Music

One extra element that might be useful for Activation level management is background music. Aim not to listen directly to the music, but for it to add a background rhythm and a tempo to your work. For example, I find familiar classical music works best to help me focus on mentally challenging work.

HOW TO IMPROVE
PERFORMANCE ACTIVATION MANAGEMENT

Let's think about pumping yourself up for a physical task like making a presentation or playing a sport. Sometimes you might need to increase your

Activation level to help you perform at your best in these types of activities.

To increase your Activation, you can use short, sharp, intense exercise, like jumping up and down on the spot. Using Focus Words (e.g., "Come on, I can do this!") and Focus Pictures (e.g., in your mind's eye seeing your Activation dial increase to the desired level) at the same time can make this even more effective. Playing some upbeat music might also help.

Reflect

If it is helpful, write down a few notes detailing what you have learned about how to better manage your Activation levels.

In this section, we've introduced many insights and techniques you can use to both increase and decrease Activation. Good DES habits will help you manage your Activation, meaning you can focus, learn, perform, and relax much more effectively.

As we move forward, you will see how good Activation habits are central for stress management, confidence, focus, being productive, performing under pressure, outstanding leadership, and ultimately becoming a Habit Mechanic and Chief Habit Mechanic.

HABIT MECHANIC LANGUAGE AND TOOL YOU HAVE LEARNED IN CHAPTER 21...

Core Language

Activation levels—A concept I've developed to make it easier to understand and manage your energy levels, alertness, and anxiety. ☑

Focus Words and Focus Pictures—Skills you can use to help control your thoughts. ☑

Planning Tool

Optimal Activation Review—A tool to help you track, compare, and improve your Activation levels through the day. ☑

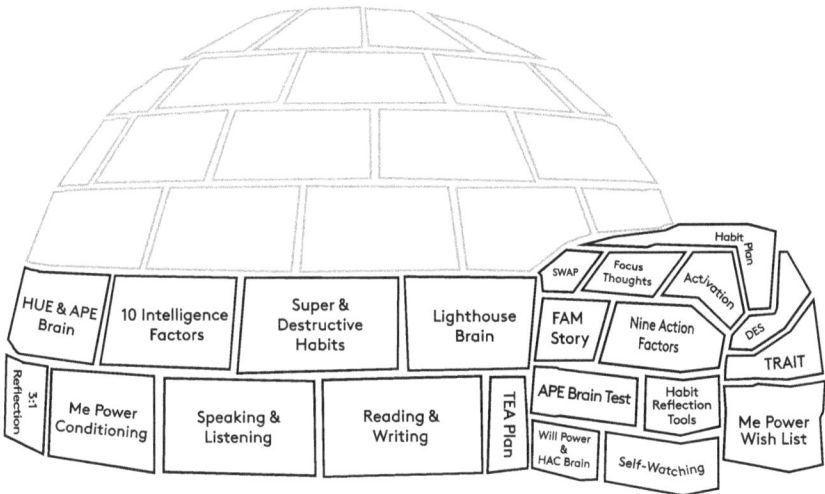

Figure 21.7: Your Habit Mechanic intelligence igloo is building up!

APPENDIX C

THE MECHANICS OF
HABIT FORMATION

W hile the main text focuses on practical Brain State optimization for the AI era, this appendix dives deeper into the science of habit formation, drawing from The Habit Mechanic. Understanding how habits work—particularly through the TRAIT (Trigger, Routine, APE Incentive, Training) framework—provides crucial insights into why Brain State optimization techniques are so powerful and how to make them automatic rather than effortful. This scientific foundation helps explain why simply knowing about AI tools isn't enough—we need to build sustainable habits around using them effectively.

17

ANALYZE AND IMPROVE
YOUR HABITS TO ACHIEVE
YOUR LONG-TERM GOALS
IN LIFE AND WORK

A TV commercial by sportswear brand Under Armour finished with the line: *"It's what you do in the dark that puts you in the light."*

It showed the world-record-breaking US swimmer Michael Phelps grinding and struggling through arduous winter training. Phelps was preparing for the 2016 Rio Olympics. It was his last appearance at the Games.

He won five gold medals and a silver, making him the most decorated Olympian of all time.

The commercial highlights the essential role your daily habits play in achieving your long-term goals.

Let's think about how habits and goals are connected.

HABITS DRIVE YOUR GOALS

Your ability to achieve your FAM (Future Ambitious Meaningful) Story will depend on your habits.

Think about the FAM Story Iceberg in a different way. Imagine you've turned the FAM Story Iceberg on its side. The tip of the iceberg, which represents your long-term future and goals, is now on the right-hand side.

The bottom of the iceberg is on the left, representing the present (today, right now) and the habits you need to develop to help you achieve your long-term goals.

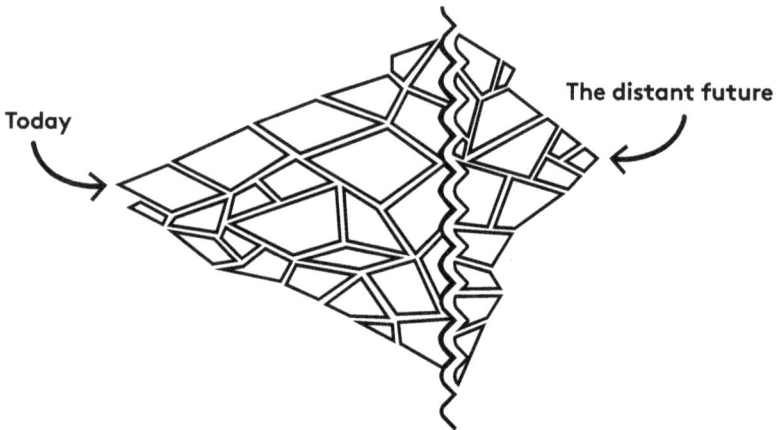

Figure 17.1: The FAM Story Iceberg tilted on its side to represent a timeline.

We all need to work on developing more helpful habits, often beginning by improving the basics like sleep, diet, and exercise.

But the challenges of the modern world mean helpful habits are not always easy to build and maintain. We need to constantly work on them.

YOUR THOUGHTS AND ACTIONS
ARE MAINLY HABIT

To help you identify which habits will help you be at your best more often, let's think about how habits work in greater depth.

First, it is important to remember that habits are all-pervading in our lives.

You will hopefully recall the statistic, which is based on the work of Professor George Lakoff from University of California, Berkeley, that at least 98 percent of all human behavior—how you think and what you do —is habit.

This means that the vast majority of what we do and think, every day, is a habit. It's also important to recognize that unhelpful thinking can be a habit.

A useful quote to help us understand just how powerful habits are in our lives is from William James—the founding father of American psychology. In his book *The Principles of Psychology, Vol.1*, he said:

"My experience of the world is what I am in the habit of attending to [doing and thinking]."

The good news is that becoming a Habit Mechanic allows you to change your habits via the process of Me Power Conditioning (deliberately working toward being your best).

INTRODUCING
THE TRAIT HABIT LOOP

To help you think in detail about how habits work, I've developed the TRAIT Habit Loop.

Figure 17.2: Other habit loops I have seen did not make perfect sense to me, so I created my own using insights from cutting-edge neuroscience and behavioral science.

Other habit models I've seen don't get to the heart of what really drives our behavior. TRAIT does, because it is based on cutting-edge science. Time and again, it has helped people develop powerful new sustainable habits.

Let me explain TRAIT in more detail.

T Is for Trigger

Triggers are the first part of the habit loop. They remind us what to do, for better or for worse.

All triggers are ultimately driven by our emotions, hence why emotional regulation is so important. But because emotions are implicit, we don't always think of them in these terms. It is easier to think of a trigger as a feeling, thought, smell, sound, or sight. Smartphones are among the most powerful triggering devices ever created. They provide endless visual, aural, and physical triggers, and are always close by.

Here is another example. Think about walking into a coffee shop. Triggers are all around you. There is high-energy, tempting, APE Brain-friendly food strategically placed when you order your drink. You might have gone to the coffee shop because you were feeling low on energy, so you will be tempted to make an impulsive purchase of a sugary treat.

R Is for Routine

Before I explain this, I want to introduce the AI (in TR**AI**T), because the Routine part of the loop will then make more sense.

AI Is for APE Incentive

The APE (Alive, Perceived, Energy) Brain is the driving force behind our behavior. So habits connected to survival, maintaining and enhancing social status, and saving energy are easy to build because these factors are most rewarding for the APE Brain. For example:

Stereotyping Is Connected to "Staying Alive"

We quickly judge—within just a tenth of a second—who is friend or foe. For example, we quickly (and possibly inaccurately) make judgments about someone we have only just met.

Thinking Habits Focusing on How You Are "Perceived by Important People"

We can mindlessly spend a lot of time thinking about what important people in our lives think about us. This can include worrying and beating ourselves up.

Thinking Habits Connected to "Conserving Energy"

We can default to high-calorie food choices when hungry or resist expending energy that does not result in a fast reward. When you feel hungry, you might eat an unhealthy sugary snack loaded with calories because it is more energy efficient than eating a piece of fruit. Or you might avoid exercise by driving to places that you could walk to. Or stop mentally challenging work to do something less mentally challenging that will consume less energy (e.g., stop writing a report to check your phone).

More on "R Is for Routine"

A trigger is always followed by a routine. The action you take, or how you think, is an automatic or semi-automatic response to the trigger. For example, your phone buzzes (trigger), you check it, see a message from your partner, and respond (routine). The routine is driven by an APE Incentive. You respond quickly to stay in your partner's good books. This might be a subconscious attempt to manage your partner's perception (the P in APE) of you (e.g., by replying quickly, you're showing them how important they are to you).

Sometimes the APE Brain can gain more than one reward from a habit. Imagine your phone buzzes on the desk while you're listening to a presentation. Your routine is to stop and check your phone. This probably takes a lot less energy (the E in APE) than concentrating on the presentation. And it might be a message from a friend that makes you feel good about yourself, rewarding the perception (the P in APE) part of the APE Brain, too (i.e., your friend must like you because they are taking the time to message you).

T Is for Training

The more you practice a habit, the more neurons in your brain become dedicated to it. More neurons make habit loops more powerful and easier to execute.

APE Brain-Friendly Habits

You can build new habits. But this ability is a double-edged sword. On one hand, it is beneficial because you can build more new helpful habits. On the other, it can be damaging because you can develop more unhelpful habits. The latter is easier than ever in the context of the VUCA world and the Learning War (described in Chapter 6).

APE Brain-friendly habits, which are typically unhelpful for modern life, are easier to build because the APE Brain is so central to the habit building process. These APE Brain-friendly habits can become addictive, meaning you continue to do them despite their negative consequences for your health, happiness, and performance. These can often be the seeds of the "Destructive Habits" that I mentioned earlier (Chapter 8, Part 7) because they unlock lots of other unhelpful habits/behaviors.

Here are some examples:

Example 1

Trigger: feeling hungry

Routine: eating an unhealthy snack that tastes good

APE Incentive: getting energy into your body—fast

Training: If this behavior is repeated often enough to become an unhelpful habit, you will gain weight, feel worse about yourself, and increase your risk of long-term health problems.

Example 2

Trigger: feeling frustrated at missing your favorite TV show because you need to go to bed

Routine: staying up late to watch the next episode

APE Incentive: It takes less energy and is more immediately rewarding to watch the next episode rather than go upstairs to bed.

Training: If this behavior is repeated often enough to become an unhelpful habit, you will not get enough sleep and will feel tired the next day, have reduced productivity, do less exercise, eat worse food, and increase your risk of long-term health problems.

Example 3

Trigger: feeling bored while doing a challenging piece of work

Routine: checking your phone

APE Incentive: It takes less energy, and is more immediately rewarding, to check your phone rather than complete your work.

Training: If this behavior is repeated often enough to become an unhelpful habit, you will have reduced productivity, need to work longer hours, become more easily distracted, and find it more difficult to do your best work.

Example 4

Trigger: feeling annoyed by something that happened at work

Routine: having a cigarette

APE Incentive: fast and energy-efficient way to relieve stress

Training: If this behavior is repeated often enough to become an unhelpful habit, you will increase your risk of long-term health problems, develop stained teeth and bad breath, and become addicted.

Example 5

Trigger: feeling stressed by your workload

Routine: drinking alcohol

APE Incentive: fast and energy-efficient way to relax

Training: If this becomes an unhelpful habit, you will have poorer sleep quality, potentially leading to poorer brain function and higher stress levels the following day. In turn, this might make it more difficult to be efficient and effective at work and lead you to eat unhealthy food, because it makes you feel better in the short-term. This will all lead to increased risks of long-term health problems.

Example 6

Trigger: feeling unhappy about yourself

Routine: buying some new clothes

APE Incentive: fast and energy-efficient way to change the way others perceive you—meaning you feel better

Training: If this behavior is repeated often enough to become an unhelpful habit, you might get deeper into debt and feel worse about yourself in the long-term.

Example 7

Trigger: You receive an email from your boss that gives you some negative feedback about your work, which your APE Brain takes personally.

Routine: beating yourself up

APE Incentive: The APE Brain is making you aware that your social status (how you are perceived by others) is under attack.

Training: If this behavior is repeated often enough to become an unhelpful habit, you will become really good at worrying about what other people think of you, become an expert in looking for personal slights or what I would call perception threats, and become an expert at beating yourself up. This might lead to long-term mental health problems.

Test?

If it is helpful, write down what TRAIT stands for to test your memory!

Reflection?

If it is helpful, why not write out one of your unhelpful habits using the TRAIT framework:

Trigger:

Routine:

APE Incentive:

Training:

HABIT MECHANIC HABIT ANALYSIS TOOLS

In-Depth Habits Reflection

Now that you understand more about how habits work, you can begin to analyze your own in more detail and do what I call an "In-Depth Habits Reflection" exercise. This builds on the APE Brain Test you completed earlier.

Remember, habits are the foundation of your FAM Story Iceberg. You will fail if your habits are not helpful to achieving your daily, weekly, and monthly goals. Creating more helpful habits will make it easier to make progress, succeed, and thrive.

To help you understand which new habits would be helpful to build this month, score yourself for each of the following statements from 1 to 10, where 1 equals "never" and 10 equals "always." Adding notes and specific examples next to statements that really resonate with you will be useful.

1. I give in to temptation and act impulsively. *Score:* _____
   Notes: _____

2. I do things I regret. *Score:* _____
   Notes: _____

3. I jump to conclusions. *Score:* _____
   Notes: _____

4. I have no discipline to keep going when things get difficult.
   Score: _____
   Notes: _____

5. I have no discipline to stay on a task and complete it. *Score:* _____
   Notes: _____

6. I stay in my comfort zone, and this stops me from being my best.
   Score: _____
   Notes: _____

7. I cannot resist temptations to quit. *Score:* _____
   Notes: _____

8. I do not continue to work when the reward is a long time in coming. *Score:* _____
   Notes: _____

9. I beat myself up when I have messed up. *Score:* _____
   Notes: _____

10. I am overconfident, and this has unhelpful consequences.
    Score: _____
    Notes: _____

11. I make excuses for my bad behavior. *Score:* _____
    Notes: _____

12. I do not push myself out of my comfort zone because I do not want to fail. *Score:* _____

    Notes: _____

13. I avoid taking personal responsibility for the quality of my own work. *Score:* _____

    Notes: _____

14. I let people down by NOT completing tasks on time to expected standards. *Score:* _____

    Notes: _____

15. I worry about things I cannot control. *Score:* _____

    Notes: _____

Now consider your scores. Identify the highest scores and the connected habits. Now, try to write down a typical way you use your most unhelpful habit, for example: "I beat myself up when I make a mistake." Don't worry if you are not sure what to write; I will help you think about your unhelpful habits in even more detail shortly.

_____

_____

_____

_____

_____

Super Habits

Now that you have reflected on some of your unhelpful habits, I want to revisit the Super Habits concept I mentioned earlier (Chapter 8, Part 7).

Through Tougher Minds' work with over 10,000 people, I repeatedly see a set of core habits (Super Habits) that seem to be more powerful than other habits in helping people be healthier, happier, and at their best.

When people develop Super Habits, many other aspects of their lives become easier because these habits trigger other helpful habits/behaviors. They enable people to manage HUE (Horribly Unhelpful Emotions) and make the type of personal progress (Habit Mechanic development) essential for feeling happy and fulfilled.

Super Habits make it easier for people to achieve the following outcomes:

1. Improving diet, exercise, and sleep for better brain performance
2. Better stress management
3. Spending less time thinking unhelpful thoughts
4. Being focused to drive productivity, creativity, and problem-solving
5. Building and maintaining robust levels of confidence
6. Performing well under pressure
7. Better leadership for improved individual and team performance

All of which lead to better work-life balance.

Finding your Super Habits will help you unlock your potential.

I have developed and refined my Super Habits over many years. They naturally develop and change as you improve your Habit Mechanic intelligence and develop more helpful habits.

Here is an overview of my current Super Habits and the other helpful habits/behaviors each one triggers. They might sound simple, but they have emerged through years of Habit Mechanic training and trial and error. Remember, there is a huge difference between knowing these things are helpful and turning them into habits.

Daily

1. **Morning run:** activates my brain and means it is easier to think clearly, focus, and be productive; triggers healthy eating habits; contributes to my overall daily exercise, which makes sleeping easier at night; helps me manage my weight.

2. **Completing a Daily TEA Plan:** makes it easier for me to get the most out of my day; triggers a lot of the productivity habits I have developed; having a productive day makes me feel better about myself at the end of the day, and helps me better manage work-life balance.

3. **Five-minute lunchtime walk where I deliberately focus on my breathing:** helps me manage stress; be productive in the after-noon; finish work on time; better manage work-life balance; sleep better.

4. **End-of-day planning for the next day, combined with a written reflection on the current day:** helps me manage stress; see progress; build confidence; finish work on time; activates my evening routine/habits, helping me sleep better.

Weekly

1. **Weekly reflection and planning for week ahead:** improves my motivation, productivity, and confidence; helps activate my daily Super Habits.

Monthly/Bimonthly

1. **Review and update my FAM (Future Ambitious Meaningful) Story:** improves my motivation, productivity, and confidence; helps activate my daily and weekly Super Habits.

2. **Complete the Team Power Leadership self-assessments (which are in Step 4 of this book):** improves my leadership; helps the business, my team, and me fulfill our potential; helps activate my daily and weekly Super Habits.

Because of life's ebbs and flows, being at our best is an ongoing journey. This means that my Super Habits are not set in stone, because I am still learning how to be my best. Also, as my life changes, I might have to adjust some of my Super Habits so they better serve me in my new life circumstances (e.g., going into the office every day versus working remotely).

It is not essential for you to understand your Super Habits right now. You will discover them over time.

The first step to uncovering your Super Habits is developing more helpful habits, in tandem with developing your Habit Mechanic intelligence. That is what this book is designed to help you do.

So, next I want you to complete an exercise designed to help you begin identifying your helpful habits. Some you will have already developed, but others you will need to purposefully build.

Helpful Habits Reflection

The "Helpful Habits Reflection" is designed to help you build on what you learned from the In-Depth Habits Reflection. This helped you think about your unhelpful habits. So at this point, it might be useful to reflect on your In-Depth Habits Reflection notes and scores.

To complete the Helpful Habits Reflection, follow these instructions:

Below are 13 statements. Read them, and choose your current position for each one from this list of three options:

> *a. Not a priority.*
> *b. I already do this well.*
> *c. I need to do this better.*

1. I reflect on my diet, exercise, and sleep, and plan to make daily improvements in these areas.
   ☐ a   ☐ b   ☐ c

2. At the end of the day, it would be helpful to reflect and highlight what went well and what I can improve tomorrow.

☐ a ☐ b ☐ c

3. At the end of every week, it would be helpful to think about what went well and to plan how I can improve next week.

☐ a ☐ b ☐ c

4. From time to time, it would be helpful to think about my future, and set long-, medium-, and short-term goals to focus my efforts and achieve my future ambitions.

☐ a ☐ b ☐ c

5. It would be helpful to regularly update my yearly and monthly calendar to add in important work and life activities.

☐ a ☐ b ☐ c

6. It would be helpful to recognize when I am stressed and successfully plan to reduce my stress.

☐ a ☐ b ☐ c

7. It would be helpful to monitor my confidence levels and successfully build up confidence in areas where it is low.

☐ a ☐ b ☐ c

8. It would be helpful to recognize when my emotions are unhelpful and successfully keep them under control.

☐ a ☐ b ☐ c

9. It would be helpful to successfully plan to improve my productivity levels.

☐ a ☐ b ☐ c

10. It would be helpful to successfully plan to improve my learning and performance in areas where I want to improve.

☐ a ☐ b ☐ c

11. It would be helpful to successfully plan to improve my performance under pressure.

    ☐ a ☐ b ☐ c

12. It would be helpful to plan out my day to improve my productivity.

    ☐ a ☐ b ☐ c

13. It would be helpful to learn how to become an even better leader.

    ☐ a ☐ b ☐ c

Now that you have reflected, give each area you have rated "c" (I need to do this better) a priority score (1 = lowest; 10 = highest).

If it is helpful, write down some reflections about what you have learned. Make a note of the helpful habits you already have that make your life easier. But also begin to consider which new helpful habits you could develop to replace your unhelpful ones.

Remember, you don't need to highlight your Super Habits yet. These will emerge over time as you develop your Habit Mechanic intelligence. The first step to uncovering your Super Habits is developing more helpful habits.

YOUR ME POWER WISH LIST

By reflecting on your habits, you will have identified the most significant challenge(s) or problem(s) your APE Brain poses. You may now wish to add any important habits you have identified to your Me Power Wish List (you started to create this in Chapter 12).

Remember, it's only realistic to make one tiny change at a time, or build one tiny new habit at a time. Nobody has the capacity to completely overhaul and change their behavior in one go. It is a gradual process.

HABIT MECHANIC LANGUAGE AND TOOLS
YOU HAVE LEARNED IN CHAPTER 17...

Core Language

TRAIT (Trigger, Routine, APE Incentive, Training) Habit Loop—
A unique habit model created to help people understand how their habits work. ☑

Self-Reflection Tools

In-Depth Habits Reflection—In-depth exercise to help you begin identifying your most unhelpful habits. ☑

Helpful Habits Reflection—An exercise to help you reflect on which new habits it would be most helpful to build. ☑

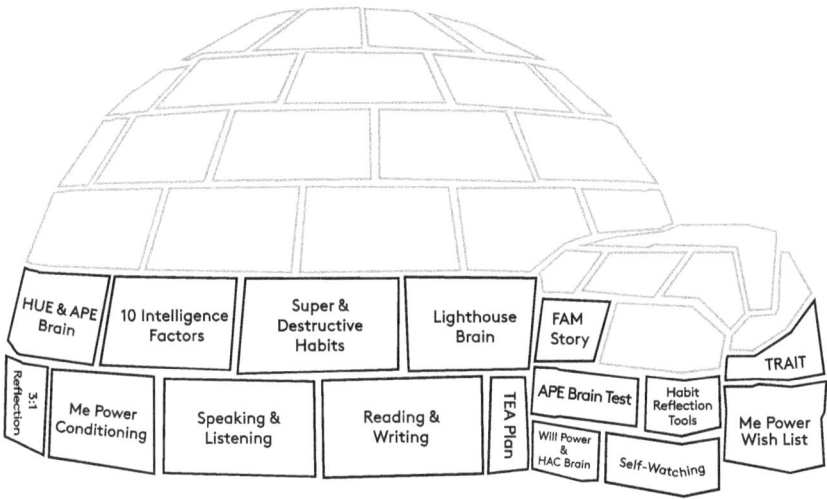

Figure 17.3: Your Habit Mechanic intelligence igloo is building up!

APPENDIX D

HOW THE NINE ACTION FACTORS FRAMEWORK BRINGS EVERYTHING TOGETHER

While the main text focuses on practical implementation of Brain State optimization, this appendix explores the deeper scientific framework behind sustainable behavior change—the Nine Action Factors model. Drawing from The Habit Mechanic, this detailed exploration shows why simply knowing about Brain States isn't enough—we need a comprehensive understanding of how habits form and change to make Brain State optimization automatic.

The story of President Obama's struggle with smoking habits illustrates a crucial truth: even highly accomplished individuals find behavior change challenging without the right scientific framework. This appendix reveals why traditional approaches to habit change mostly fail, and how understanding these nine fundamental factors can transform how effectively you implement Brain State optimization practices.

18

THE SECRET NINE FACTORS THAT REALLY CONTROL YOUR LIFE

I f we did not already recognize that it is challenging for anyone to build new helpful habits, a story about former US president Barack Obama can help us understand more. It is also worth noting that Obama was not just the first African American president but the third youngest in over 100 years.

CBS News showed Mr. Obama taking questions from the press shortly after announcing new laws to regulate the American tobacco industry. A reporter asked him several questions about his own smoking habits. How many cigarettes does he smoke every day? Does he smoke in the presence of others?

Barack Obama is regarded by many as a consummate statesman, a highly capable leader, and a powerful role model. But even he admitted that stopping smoking was a "struggle." "Have I fallen off the wagon?" he said. "Occasionally, yes."

He added: "I'd say I am 95 percent cured, but there are times when I mess up. Like folks who go to Alcoholics Anonymous…smoking is something you continually struggle with."

In this chapter, we'll explore the science and the simple practice steps you can use to build the sustainable new habits that will make it easier to be your best.

VERBAL PERSUASION DOESN'T WORK!

Changing our habits (the foundations of all human behavior) is complex. We often fail because we do not understand the science of behavioral change.

When we try to build a new habit in any area of our life, the default (but faulty) behavior change technique we have been taught is what I term "verbal persuasion."

We notice an unhelpful habit and persuade ourselves we really DO need to stop. For example, we tell ourselves, "We are beating ourselves up too much…we must stop." We may even tell somebody else of our intention to stop this unhelpful behavior.

We use the same verbal persuasion technique if we want someone else to change a behavior. You might say: "I think it would be a good idea if you turned up for meetings on time, because this would be helpful for team performance." But even if people agree that your behavior change suggestion is a good idea, this is not enough to help people build the new habits that will deliver the change.

The behavioral science is clear: this traditional approach to changing our habits is overreliant on Will Power. Wanting to make a change is not enough to build a new habit. To make sustainable change, we must use insights from behavioral science to create a precise step-by-step approach.

WILL POWER IS THE CONDUIT FOR CHANGE—
BUT IT IS LIMITED

All behavior change begins with using Will Power to resist the old habit. For example:

Trigger and APE Incentive: You notice the urge to check your phone, NOW, meaning you will have to break your focus on an important piece of work you need to complete ASAP. This is HUE (Horribly Unhelpful Emotions) looking for short-term gratification—driven by the *APE Incentive*. Having the phone in your eyeline is part of the *trigger* for your desire to check it.

Routine: You use Will Power to regulate your emotions and resist the temptation of entering the old routine of checking the phone. By doing this, you are starting to create a new routine, that is, when you feel the urge to check your phone, you show resolve and stay focused on the task on which you are working.

But if you only rely on your Will Power, it is likely HUE will eventually win and you will check your phone.

Although Will Power is the conduit for building new helpful habits, it is a limited resource. So we need to use Will Power PLUS behavioral science to secure new habits.

THE NINE ACTION FACTORS FRAMEWORK

To help people regulate their emotions and supercharge the habit building process, I used the latest insights from behavioral science to create the proprietary Tougher Minds "Nine Action Factors" framework. I use this framework, and the 200+ tactics I have created, to help my clients create personal and cultural change (i.e., a habit building program across a team or entire business). Here I will show you how to use a simple version to help you build new habits that last.

All of the nine factors are interconnected. Each is also connected to the TRAIT (Trigger, Routine, APE Incentive, Training) Habit Loop. Here is a simple overview of the nine factors (I will explain each in greater detail later):

1. Habit Mechanic Mindset Factor (*APE Incentive*)

**Habit Mechanic
Mindset**

Figure 18.1: If you don't believe you can improve, you never will.
The right mindset is essential for changing your habits.

2. Brain State Optimization Factor (*Training*; *APE Incentive*)

Brain State

Figure 18.2: To successfully build new habits, your brain
needs to be neurobiologically ready for change.

3. Tiny Changes Factor (*APE Incentive*)

Tiny Changes

Figure 18.3: You can change but only one tiny step at a time.

4. Personal Motivation Factor (*APE Incentive*)

**Personal
Motivation**

Figure 18.4: It is easier to change if there is a meaningful reason why.

5. Personal Knowledge and Skills Factor (*Routine*)

**Personal Knowledge
& Skills**

Figure 18.5: Building new habits often requires you to learn new things.

6. Community Knowledge and Skills Factor (*Routine*)

**Community
Knowledge & Skills**

*Figure 18.6: If the people around you already know how to do the thing you
want to learn (e.g., manage stress), it will be easier for you to learn it.*

7. Social Influence Factor (*APE Incentive*)

Social Influence

*Figure 18.7: If the people around you are already doing the thing
you want to do, it will be easier for you to do it.*

8. Rewards and Penalties Factor (*APE Incentive*)

Rewards & Penalties

Figure 18.8: Rewards encourage behavior and penalties discourage it.

9. External Triggers Factor (*Trigger*)

Physical & Digital

Figure 18.9: It is easier to do things if you get triggered (reminded) to do them.

Figure 18.10: Activating all Nine Action Factors together makes building and sustaining new habits easier.

WHY DO WE NEED TO KNOW SO MUCH TO BUILD NEW HELPFUL HABITS?

Many of the thoughts and actions that are unhelpful for our health, happiness, and performance are what I call *simple behaviors*, like eating donuts, checking your phone too often, and beating yourself up. These behaviors are APE (Alive, Perceived, Energy) Brain–friendly and driven by human instincts connected to staying alive, achieving and maintaining social status, and conserving energy. These simple behaviors are increasingly agitated and exploited in the Learning War we are all fighting.

Unfortunately, many of the thoughts and actions that are most helpful for being our best in the modern world are what I call *complex behaviors*, like sleeping well, eating healthily, exercising sufficiently, not dwelling on negatives for too long, and becoming an outstanding leader. These behaviors are not APE Brain–friendly. They require us to learn new knowledge and skills and become expert habit builders or, in other words, Habit Mechanics and Chief Habit Mechanics.

The Nine Action Factors are constantly influencing your behavior (for better and for worse), but we are largely unaware of them. To help you take more control over your own thoughts and actions, I'll show you how to use the Nine Action Factors framework to your advantage.

USING THE NINE ACTION FACTORS

I use learning to drive as an example to understand more about how we can use the Nine Action Factors to help us build new helpful habits. Just like many of the things we would like to improve, driving is also a *complex behavior*, which is why it is a good example to use. Even if you haven't learned how to drive, this example will still make sense. Here are the nine factors and how they influence us when we learn to drive.

1. Habit Mechanic Mindset

Think of mindset as belief and what we believe. People with a *Habit Mechanic Mindset* believe they can improve anything with practice and take responsibility for being their best. People with an *APE Brain Mindset* believe they are only good at certain things, cannot change, and become victims of VUCA World Conditioning (Chapter 9, Figure 9.1). If we did not believe we could learn to drive and were not prepared to put the effort into learning, we would not have achieved this milestone. A Habit Mechanic Mindset is essential for learning to drive.

(To learn more about the origins of how I began to understand this factor, start with Professor Carol Dweck's work on mindset and Professor Walter Mischel's work on mastering your mindset by understanding your self-control, and see how these theories have developed over time.)

2. Brain State Optimization

In simple terms, this relates to how ready your brain is to learn. If you were sleep-deprived and took a driving lesson, you would unlikely be in the right Brain State to concentrate or gain anything helpful from the lesson. Equally, if you are stressed or in a bad mood, it will also be more difficult to learn. Remember: emotion drives attention; attention drives learning.

If we want to learn something new, we must be in the right Brain State.

(To learn more about the origins of how I began to understand this factor, start with Professor John Medina's "Brain Rules" work.)

3. Tiny Changes

This factor relates to the size or scale of the change we want to make (e.g., lose 15 pounds, get an extra hour of sleep per night, become the best leader in my business). In simple terms, we can make changes to behavior, but we can only make one tiny change at a time. If we want to learn to do something new, it is far more efficient to do it in stages and focus on making one tiny change at a time. For example, we learn to drive over extended periods and build a surprising amount of tiny new interconnected habits. We do not simply climb in the car and immediately gain a complete understanding of how to drive. Often, many first lessons just involve the student working out where all the controls are in the vehicle.

So, to best use the Tiny Factor, we should work toward an accumulation of tiny changes and improvements, instead of trying to make a single massive leap of progress. Here are some other examples:

- Want to lose one stone (or 14 pounds)? First focus on losing half a pound.
- Want to get an extra hour of sleep per night? Aim for one minute of extra sleep tonight, then build up to five minutes and so on.
- Want to be the best leader in your business? Start by building one tiny new habit that will improve your leadership.

In this book, I've deliberately used **"tiny" and "small" interchangeably**.

(To learn more about the origins of how I began to understand this factor, start with Professor BJ Fogg's work on tiny habits and see how these theories have developed over time.)

4. Personal Motivation

It's easier to make a change or build a new habit if you can connect it to a bigger meaningful goal in your life. This is one of the reasons why I asked you to create a FAM (Future Ambitious Meaningful) Story Iceberg (Chapter 16).

In the case of driving, you may have needed or wanted to learn how for work reasons, or to take your children to school, or to be the first qualified driver in your peer group, or some other reason. If we can connect the change we want to make to our bigger goals, dreams, and desires, this will provide motivation and make it easier to keep persisting with difficult changes.

(To learn more about the origins of how I began to understand this factor, start with Professor Edwin A. Locke's, and Professor Edward Deci and Professor Richard Ryan's, work on motivation and self-determination and see how these theories have developed over time.)

5. Personal Knowledge and Skills

We do not need to acquire new knowledge and skills to eat a donut, but it is often essential for complex behavior change—like learning to drive, improving our confidence, or enhancing our sleep or productivity, etc.

(To learn more about the origins of how I began to understand this factor, start with Professor Anders Ericsson's work on expertise and see how these theories have developed over time.)

6. Community Knowledge and Skills

What knowledge and skills do our families, peers, and communities have that might help us? Having a parent who knows how to drive can be helpful if you also want to learn (think of free driving lessons in supermarket car parks). A colleague knowing how to build better stress management habits is helpful if you also want to develop some.

The reason I try to make all our insights simple is so they can be easily shared among colleagues and families and across the Habit Mechanic community. The more people there are in your network who understand the Habit Mechanic Tools and language, the more powerful they become.

(To learn more about the origins of how I began to understand this factor, start with Professor Albert Bandura's work on social learning and see how this theory has developed over time.)

7. Social Influence

Our APE Brain is strongly influenced by the behavior of those people we look up to and respect. Remember, P stands for Perceived. So we implicitly worry about how we are perceived by these people because we want them to like us. In the case of learning to drive, if our parents think that speed limits can be ignored or there is no need for car insurance, they won't be good *role models* for us as learner drivers.

(To learn more about the origins of how I began to understand this factor, start with Dr. Stanley Milgram's and Professor Robert Cialdini's respective work on social influence and see how these theories have developed over time.)

8. Rewards and Penalties

Our APE Brain is strongly influenced by rewards and penalties. These can be social, intrinsic, or extrinsic. In the case of driving, people are rewarded for driving well and penalized for driving poorly. If you drive well, you will eventually pass your test and gain a full license (a reward). A long period of accident-free driving usually means a lower motor insurance premium (another reward). But breaking the speed limit can mean a fine, points, higher insurance, and, if you do it too many times, a lost license (in other words, penalties!). We can use rewards and penalties to help us build new helpful habits.

(To learn more about the origins of how I began to understand this factor, start with Professor B. F. Skinner's work on variable rewards and see how these theories have developed over time.)

9. External Triggers

External triggers in our modern world can be physical and digital. The smartphone is one of the most powerful external triggers ever designed. In a vehicle, we are surrounded by triggers. The speedometer shows us how fast we are traveling. A line in the middle of the road indicates which side we should drive on. A pedestrian crossing will remind us to stop. All of these are triggers, and they are often loaded with rewards and penalties. I will explain more about this later.

(To learn more about the origins of how I began to understand this factor, start with Professor Richard Thaler and Professor Cass Sunstein's "nudge" work and see how these theories have developed over time.)

SUMMARY OF THE NINE ACTION FACTORS

Think of each factor like a switch that you can turn on or off. If you "turn the switch on" for each factor, they will work for you, and building a new habit will become easier. But if the "switches are turned off," each factor will work against you, and building the habit will be more difficult. Learning how to turn each switch on is an essential Habit Mechanic skill, and something you will be much better at by the time you finish the book.

Test?

If it is helpful, write down the Nine Action Factors to see how good your memory is!

LEARNING HOW TO "SWITCH ON" THE NINE ACTION FACTORS

How Can I Learn to Develop a Habit Mechanic Mindset?

You are already developing one by reading this book. First, you are learning about science-based insights that show your abilities are not fixed and that you can change and improve. Second, you are learning how to build small new helpful habits so you can directly experience positive personal change. For example, if you have been using the Daily TEA Plan regularly, I would imagine you are already starting to see some success. This will build your confidence in your ability to make changes that help you feel and perform better.

How Can I Learn to Optimize My Brain State?

Start by using the insights shared in:

- Chapter 19 to improve your sleep, diet, and exercise habits
- Chapter 21 to improve your Activation
- Chapter 22 to improve your stress management
- Chapter 23 to calm your brain by building robust confidence
- Chapter 25 to supercharge your focus and productivity

These insights will help you become an expert at optimizing your Brain State, making it easier for you to build new habits and be your best.

Will You Remind Me to Focus On Making Tiny Changes?

Yes. This idea is built into the Habit Mechanic self-reflection and planning tools within this book, for example, Daily TEA (*Tiny* Empowering Action) Plan.

How Can I Learn to Increase My
Personal Motivation?

The Future Ambitious Meaningful (FAM) Story (Chapter 16) has been purposely designed to help you do this and has already helped thousands of other Habit Mechanics fire up their motivation.

An important motivation theory embedded into the Habit Mechanic self-reflection and planning tools is called self-determination. I will explain more about this and how to use it in "The Cultural Architect" (Chapter 32).

How Can I Learn the Knowledge and Skills to Help
Me Develop the Habits I Want to Build?

If you want to develop habits to help you achieve the following outcomes, I am going to show you how throughout the remainder of the book.

- Improving diet, exercise, and sleep for better brain health and performance (Chapter 19)
- Better stress management (Chapter 22)
- Spending less time thinking unhelpful thoughts (Chapters 22 and 23)
- Being focused to drive productivity, creativity, and problem-solving (Chapter 25)
- Building and maintaining robust levels of confidence (Chapter 23)
- Performing well under pressure (Chapter 24)
- Better leadership for improved individual and team performance (Step 4—Chief Habit Mechanic skills)

To turn these insights into **Community Knowledge and Skills** (the sixth Action Factor), share what you have learned and encourage others to become Habit Mechanics.

How Can I Learn More about Using
the Social Influence Factor?

In the "Chief Habit Mechanic skills" section (Step 4), you will learn more about:

- How people influence each other's behavior and habits
- How you can get better at influencing others by becoming a Team Power Leader
- How you can develop other Team Power Leaders who also positively influence other people's behavior in your team, group, or organization

How Can I Learn More about Using the
Reward and Penalty Factor?

There are lots of "reward and penalty systems" deliberately built into the self-reflection and planning tools in this book. However, explaining the nuances of all of these is beyond the scope of this book. But I do want to spend a little bit of time explaining how you can deliberately create reward and penalty systems to help you build new habits.

"Carrot (reward) and stick (penalty)" is probably the most popular phrase used to explain this factor. But this phrase oversimplifies the complex inner workings of your brain. As I explained earlier, the APE Incentive component of the TRAIT Habit Loop drives your behavior. So when we are thinking about rewards and penalties, we must think in terms of what is rewarding for the APE Brain and what is not. I covered some of the basics of APE Incentives in the example APE Brain–friendly habits detailed in Chapter 17. Some of the key words used to describe APE Incentives were "using less energy," "immediate rewards," and "energy efficient," which is no surprise since your brain is designed to conserve energy. But now let's dig a little deeper to learn what else your APE Brain finds rewarding.

Familiar Reward and Penalty Systems

It is important to recognize the **reward and penalty systems** that influence our day-to-day lives. For example, why don't you speed when driving? There could be several answers to this question:

- I want to be a responsible citizen.
- I don't want to get a speeding fine or risk the cost of my car insurance increasing.
- Losing my license would be embarrassing.

Your answer could be a combination of the above, or a range of other answers. But broadly they will fall into three categories:

1. Intrinsic—how it makes me feel (e.g., being a responsible citizen makes me feel good).
2. Extrinsic—what I will get (e.g., cheaper car insurance saves me money).
3. Social—what people will think of me (e.g., losing my driving license might make people think less of me).

Some of your answers might fall into more than one category (e.g., being a responsible citizen makes you feel good [intrinsic] and might make others think you are a good person [social]).

Reward and penalty systems are built into our societies through laws that are designed to encourage people to behave in a way that is beneficial for society. Rules of conduct are used in a similar way at school, at work, and in other groups. For example, if you go to work, you get paid (reward).

Reward and penalty systems are also built into the products and services businesses are trying to sell you. It is said that all products and services can be put into three broad and overarching categories:

1. Health
2. Wealth
3. Relationships

If you purchase the product or service, it will increase one or more of these areas (reward), but if you don't make the purchase nothing will change (penalty).

Understanding this is helpful, because you can reflect on which laws, rules, and products or services (or reward and penalty systems) were, or are, most successful in influencing your behavior—and which are not. Further, you can begin to consider why some reward and penalty systems have more impact on your behavior than others. This will help you begin thinking about how you can better use rewards and penalties to help you build new habits.

The Secret Science of Achievement

We are hardwired to find improving and achieving both rewarding and motivational. For example, if you are on a diet and you are losing weight, it is easier to keep going because the feeling of achieving (or making progress) gives your brain a dopamine hit. However, if you step on the scale and you have gained weight, you are more likely to feel like giving up because you don't feel the efforts you are putting into changing yourself are paying off.

In simple terms, you get a brain reward (a prolonged hit of dopamine) when you feel like you are making progress, but a brain penalty (your dopamine levels and mood are lowered) when you are not.

Practical Actions

Set tiny goals—By setting tiny goals (remember the Tiny Factor) that are easy to achieve, you will more likely make progress, feel good, and keep going. For example, one minute of extra sleep tonight; five minutes of extra walking today; do one sit-up; write down one positive about your day at the end of each day. If you persist with tiny changes, they become the foundations of bigger results. For example, losing half-a-pound per week soon adds up to losing a significant amount of weight; starting with one minute of extra sleep per night can eventually result in gaining extra hours of sleep per week; five minutes of extra walking per day turns into extra miles every week; one sit-up per day quickly turns into 20 per day; one positive reflection each day turns into a more positive outlook on life.

Track your progress—Setting and reviewing your goals makes it easier to see the progress you are making. Also, if you notice you are not achieving the desired results, you can adjust your goals to make them easier to achieve and create some positive change momentum.

This book is packed full of Habit Mechanic Tools to help you monitor your progress. Here is another, which I call the "Me Power Weekly Wall Chart." I created it to help me plan for the week. I fill it in and stick it on my fridge at the beginning of each week.

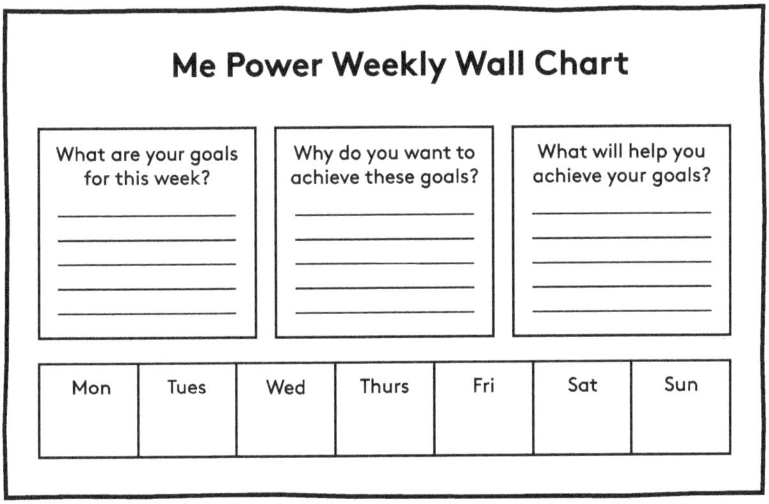

Figure 18.11: Me Power Weekly Wall Chart

It has built-in reward and penalty systems. Here's how it works.

1. First, make a list of your goals for the week.
2. Next, answer the question, "Why do you want to achieve these goals?"
3. Then answer the question, "What will help you achieve these goals?"
4. Each day you achieve what you wanted to achieve, give yourself a tick (or a cross if you fail).
5. Aim to get as many consecutive ticks as possible, and create a "tick streak" (i.e., an unbroken run of days with a tick).
6. Set a new record for creating a tick streak (e.g., my previous personal best unbroken run was 3 days, now I want to break that record by achieving 4 days).
7. Finally, keep setting new records by breaking your longest tick streak.

To make it easier to complete, I have created a PDF template. I use this, and if you want to use it go to tougherminds.co.uk/habitmechanic and click on "Resources" to download your copy.

Gamification

By using something like the Me Power Weekly Wall Chart, you are beginning to gamify your reward and penalty systems. You can of course go much further (think "likes," points, badges, leaderboards, etc.). These techniques and others are what your favorite games, apps, restaurants, and brands increasingly use to hook you into coming back time and again.

Other techniques used are

- scarcity (sale, happy hour, buy-one-get-one-free offers, only limited places available);

- unpredictability (making a bet, scratch cards, playing the lottery, product drops); and
- loss (fear of missing out, breaking your longest streak, losing all your data if you unsubscribe, countdown timers to encourage you not to miss out on this fantastic offer).

All these tactics are being used against you every day in the Learning War.

The more knowledge you have of these reward and penalty systems, the better you will be able to use them to your advantage in building the habits that help you be your best. So I hope these introductory reward and penalty insights provide a good starting point for you.

How Can I Learn More about Using the External Triggers Factor?

The good news is you already have. For example, the Me Power Weekly Wall Chart is an external trigger (if you print it out and stick it in a prominent place). And like all powerful triggers, it doubles as a reward and penalty system.

Examples from Your Smartphone

What are the most powerful external triggers ever designed? I would argue that smartphones and watches are among them. This is because they are deliberately loaded with rewards and penalties, and are always very close by/ strapped to you! A report by BBC News editor James Reevell detailed some of the science used by phone companies to get us hooked on their devices. He focused on several areas.

The "Dot Dot Dot" That Comes Up When You're Waiting For Someone to Reply to Your Text

This is designed to induce a small stress and dopamine response (dopamine is released in anticipation of a reward). It is connected to the "unpredictability" gamification idea I mentioned above. It is also called a "variable reward."

"Like" Buttons on Our Social Media Apps

This feeds directly into the APE Brain's subconscious concerns about how much other people like us.

Red Notification Dots

Most of us have been conditioned to relate red to mean danger, stop, and pay attention. So seeing the red dot can create a little stress response in your brain that compels you to take action (e.g., check the message NOW, because it could be an important one!).

Speed Camera Lottery

Another great example of an external trigger with a supercharged reward and penalty system is Kevin Richardson's speed camera lottery idea. Speed cameras already contain a powerful reward and penalty system, but Richardson took it a step further. He wanted to provide extra incentives for obeying the speed limit.

Here's how it works: Speeders get fined and money goes into a pot. If you are obeying the speed limit, your details will also be recorded and you will be entered into a lottery to have a chance of winning some of the money paid in fines by those who broke the speed limit.

Hot Triggers

When I was a teenager, I worked for one of the biggest fast-food companies on the planet. Back then, people had to physically come into the restaurant to buy their burger and fries. But that is not the case anymore. People can now use an app to order at home while sitting on their couch. So the fast-food companies' advertisements, whether on TV or the internet, have become what psychologists would call "hot triggers."

Remember, triggers are the first part of the habit loop. They remind you what to do. But some are more powerful than others.

When I was a teenager, a TV ad for a fast-food company might have reminded me that I liked their food. But it would not have compelled me to get up, go out of the house, and walk to their closest outlet (one mile away) to go and buy the food. It was too much effort.

But these new ads are hot triggers because they tell your APE Brain what to do right now (order some food via your smartphone), knowing that you can immediately place an order on your phone and the food will be with you within 30 minutes.

Also note that companies continually change their ads to keep them fresh—otherwise they become boring and less interesting to your APE Brain. Remember, it likes fun, exciting, new things.

Here are some other examples of hot triggers:

- Your phone buzzing in your pocket
- A piece of chocolate cake in your fridge (the place you look when you are hungry!)
- The seat belt alert noise to remind you to put it on

Why am I telling you this? Hot triggers have a powerful effect on what you do, and if you are aware of them, it is easier to make them work for you. For example, if your phone keeps distracting you when you are trying to complete a piece of work, turn it off and put it out of sight. If you want to create a Daily TEA Plan at the beginning of each day, print out the PDF and put it in a place where you will see it first thing (e.g., your desk).

If you have not already, go to <u>tougherminds.co.uk/habitmechanic</u> and click on "Resources" to download your copy of the Daily TEA Plan PDF.

Also, keep your hot triggers fresh. For example, I create bespoke monthly planners for some of my clients. But every month my designers create a new planner cover to make the planner more interesting for those using it.

ACTIVATING THE NINE
ACTION FACTORS TOGETHER

You will be far more successful in building new habits if you plan to use all Nine Action Factors together. To help you do this, I have created the "Habit Building Plan," which I will show you how to use shortly.

> *But first we'll look at how you can begin to build better diet, exercise, and sleep habits to boost your brain health and performance.*

HABIT MECHANIC LANGUAGE YOU HAVE
LEARNED IN CHAPTER 18...

Core Language

Nine Action Factors framework—Created to make it easy for you to use the latest insights from behavioral science to build sustainable new habits. ☑

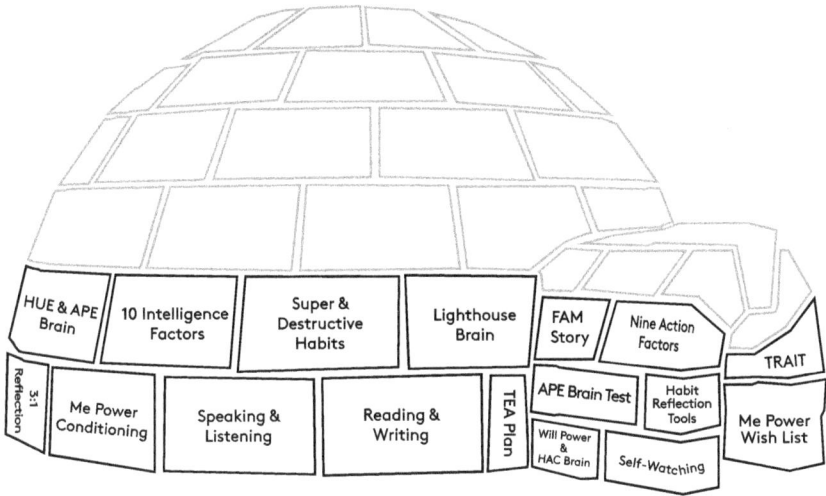

Figure 18.12: Your Habit Mechanic intelligence igloo is building up!

Text within the figure:

HUE & APE Brain

10 Intelligence Factors

Super & Destructive Habits

Lighthouse Brain

FAM Story

Nine Action Factors

TRAIT

3:1 Reflection

Me Power Conditioning

Speaking & Listening

Reading & Writing

TEA Plan

APE Brain Test

Will Power & HAC Brain

Habit Reflection Tools

Self-Watching

Me Power Wish List

ACKNOWLEDGMENTS

This book would not have been possible without the support, wisdom, and encouragement of many remarkable people who have shaped both my thinking and the Brain State optimization approach I share in these pages.

First, I must thank my extraordinary team who helped develop and refine the Success Cycle and the Brain State framework: Andrew Foster, Catherine Grant, Professor Jim McKenna, Andrew Whitelam, and Dr. Laura Lucia Rossi. Your insights, challenges, and unwavering belief in this work have been invaluable.

To the over 20,000 professionals and 100s of organizations who have trusted my team and me to help them navigate the unprecedented challenges of the modern world—thank you for allowing us to learn alongside you. Your courage in embracing these new approaches, your candid feedback, and your remarkable results continue to inspire and inform everything we do.

This work stands on the shoulders of giants in the fields of neuroscience, behavioral science, and performance psychology. I am deeply grateful to all the researchers and practitioners whose groundbreaking work I've drawn upon, including Professors Barbara Fredrickson, George Lakoff, Daniel Kahneman, John Arden, and many others whose dedication to understanding the human brain has made this practical approach possible.

Special thanks to the publishing team who helped bring this book to life, including Caerus. Your commitment to excellence and attention to detail have made all the difference.

To my family and friends who have supported me through the intense periods of research and writing that made this book possible—thank you for your patience, encouragement, and understanding.

Finally, to my early teachers and coaches who first ignited my passion for understanding human potential and performance—your influence continues to shape my work and my life. You showed me that mastering our minds is humanity's most vital skill, a truth that becomes ever more apparent as we navigate the AI revolution together.

Dr. Jon Finn

BIBLIOGRAPHY

I am fortunate to be able to stand on the shoulders of many groundbreaking scientists who dedicated their lives to developing some of the insights that underpin the 'Habit Mechanic AI-Edge' approach. I have mentioned some of them throughout the course of this book, but also provide an overview of some specific research papers and books that have influenced my thinking over the years in the online bibliography. To access it, go to <u>tougherminds. co.uk/trainyourbrain</u> and click on "Bibliography."

QUICK RECAP INDEX